Greed, Lust and Power: Franciscan Strategies for Building a More Just World

Washington Theological Union
Symposium Papers
2010

GREED, LUST AND POWER: FRANCISCAN STRATEGIES FOR BUILDING A MORE JUST WORLD

WASHINGTON THEOLOGICAL UNION SYMPOSIUM PAPERS
2010

EDITED BY

DARIA MITCHELL, O.S.F.

THE FRANCISCAN INSTITUTE
ST. BONAVENTURE UNIVERSITY
ST. BONAVENTURE, NEW YORK

© Franciscan Institute Publications
St. Bonaventure University
St. Bonaventure, NY 14778
2011
CFIT/ESC-OFM Series
Number 10

The articles in this book were originally presented at a symposium sponsored by the Franciscan Center
at Washington Theological Union, Washington, DC,
May 28-30, 2010

This publication is the tenth in a series of documents
resulting from the work of the
Commission on the Franciscan Intellectual Tradition
of the English-speaking Conference
of the Order of Friars Minor. (CFIT/ESC-OFM)

Cover design: Jennifer L. Davis

ISBN 10: 1-57659-220-0
ISBN 13: 978-1-57659-220-5

Library of Congress Control Number
2010941996

Printed and bound in the United States of America.

BookMasters, Inc.
Ashland, OH

TABLE OF CONTENTS

ABBREVIATIONS

CA:ED   *Clare of Assisi: Early Documents, The Lady.* Edited and translated by Regis J. Armstrong. New York: New City Press, 2006.

FA:ED   *Francis of Assisi: Early Documents*, Volumes 1-3. Edited by Regis Armstrong, J.A. Wayne Hellmann, William Short. New York: New City Press, 1999-2001.

NEW TESTAMENT

MATT	1 COR	1 THES	HEBR	3 JOHN
MARK	2 COR	2 THES	JAMES	JUDE
LUKE	GAL	1 TIM	1 PETER	REV
JOHN	EPH	2 TIM	2 PETER	
ACTS	PHIL	TITUS	1 JOHN	
ROM	COL	PHLM	2 JOHN	

THE WRITINGS OF SAINT FRANCIS

Adm	The Admonitions
BlL	A Blessing for Br. Leo
CtC	The Canticle of the Creatures
CtExh	The Canticle of Exhortation
1Frg	Fragments of Worchester Manuscript
2Frg	Fragments of Thomas of Celano
3Frg	Fragments from Hugh of Digne
LtAnt	A Letter to Br. Anthony of Padua
1LtCl	The First Letter to the Clergy (Early Edition)
2LtCl	The Second Letter to the Clergy (Later Edition)
1LtCus	The First Letter to the Custodians
2LtCus	The Second Letter to the Custodians
1LtF	The First Letter to the Faithful
2LtF	The Second Letter to the Faithful

LtL	A Letter to Br. Leo
LtMin	A Letter to a Minister
LtOrd	A Letter to the Entire Order
LtR	A Letter to Rulers of the Peoples
ExhP	Exhortation to the Praise of God
PrOF	A Prayer Inspired by the Our Father
PrsG	The Praises of God
OfP	The Office of the Passion
PrCr	The Prayer before the Crucifix
ER	The Earlier Rule (Regula non bullata)
LR	The Later Rule (Regula bullata)
RH	A Rule for Hermitages
SalBVM	A Salutation of the Blessed Virgin Mary
SalV	A Salutation of Virtues
Test	The Testament
TPJ	True and Perfect Joy

WRITINGS OF SAINT CLARE

1LAg	First Letter to Agnes of Prague
2LAg	Second Letter to Agnes of Prague
3LAg	Third Letter to Agnes of Prague
4LAg	Fourth Letter to Agnes of Prague
LEr	Letter to Ermentrude of Bruges
RCl	Rule of St. Clare
TestCl	Testament of St. Clare
BCl	Blessing of St. Clare

FRANCISCAN SOURCES

1C	The Life of St. Francis by Thomas of Celano
2C	The Remembrance of the Desire of a Soul
3C	The Treatise on the Miracles by Thomas of Celano
Lch	The Legend for Use in Choir
Off	The Divine Office of St. Francis by Julian of Speyer
LJS	The Life of St. Francis by Julian of Speyer
VL	The Versified Life of St. Francis by Henri d'Avranches
1-3JT	The Praises by Jacopone da Todi

PREFACE

More than one participant in this year's Symposium told me, tongue-in-cheek, that she/he could not wait to hear what our presenters would say about *these* strategies. What they did hear, in exchanges that make the annual Franciscan Symposium an experience as nourishing for the spirit as it is for the mind, were poignant descriptions of the world in which we live and, what is more, challenging proposals as to how we may confront this world from the heart of a Tradition whose members walk in the footprints of the One who came not to "condemn the world, but that the world might be saved through him (John 3:17)." As St. Francis of Assisi admonished his brothers in their *Earlier Rule* (XVII, 19): "When we see or hear evil spoken or done or God blasphemed, let us speak well and do well and praise God *Who is blessed forever* (Rom 1:25)."

The fulfillment of such an admonition is no easy task. It demands that we enter into that process of *conscientization* which one of the Symposium's presenters described as an engagement of our world – our nation, our Church, and our own Franciscan Family – that is both informed by the teachings of the Gospel and guided by the principles of social analysis: observe, judge, and act. In this way, we are able to discern what our Franciscan responses to the needs of a world infected by greed, lust, and disordered uses of power should be, and so develop strategies capable of affecting those responses. As our guides in this process of conscientization exemplified the distinctly Franciscan strategies they would develop and present to this Symposium's participants.

Joseph Nangle, O.F.M. is a former missionary to Bolivia and Peru who brings his experience as a reverse-missionary to the United States to bear in the Symposium's opening presentation.

In his talk, Nangle sets the stage, so to speak, for the talks that follow. He calls upon all the Symposium's participants to accept the challenge of conscientization, and dare look upon our world with new eyes.

In his first hypothesis, Nangle argues that to understand the United States and its place among the family of nations correctly, we must understand it as an empire, an empire that, in spite of the many "wholesome features of our society ... the description by Pope John Paul II and more recently Pope Benedict XVI of ours as a 'culture of death' rings true." Nangle concludes with a challenge that flows from this understanding: "We surely did not choose this here and now for ourselves; we may not even wish to be part of it. But the fact is that accepting the truth of this hypothesis, gives us no choice but to deal with this modern version of empire from our Christian and Franciscan traditions."

In his second and third hypotheses, Nangle draws out the consequences of this twofold challenge. Traditionally Franciscan scholarship and spirituality "generally tend to face the past in addressing the present and the future." Nangle challenges Franciscans to turn their faces toward the future and "do a better job of 'connecting the historical dots' between the rich and truly cutting edge tradition which is ours and twenty-first century American life as described in the first hypothesis."

Flowing from this, Nangle offers his third hypothesis, that Franciscans tend not to look outside their own worldview when searching for strategies to build a more just world. He challenges Franciscan men and women to form partnerships with practitioners of other spiritual traditions and the social sciences. Only by means of such partnerships, Nangle concludes, will Franciscans be able "to translate our charism into a real contribution to all the wonderful work being done today on behalf of Justice, Peace and the Integrity of Creation."

The next presentation by author, activist, and popular scholar Michael Crosby, O.F.M. Cap., Ph.D., follows seamlessly upon that of Nangle. Crosby engages the insights of others laboring for a more just world in order to establish his thesis: "the vices and sins of lust and greed are the result of appropriating something good (i.e. sexuality and wealth) in ways that represent an abuse not only of power but of relationships that create authentic community. As a result only an individual and communal stance of non-appropriation, 'purity of heart' and trusting relationships will serve as an antidote to their controlling power."

In the first section of his presentation, Crosby draws upon the work of Robert Bellah, Wendell Berry, Thomas Cahil, S.V.D., and Joseph Chinnici, O.F.M. to demonstrate how the deadly sins of greed and lust use power to appropriate all human relationships for the service of the selfish and covetous desires of those who wield it. It was in the face of just such a violent use of power that Francis of Assisi established a form of life he called "walking in the footprints of Jesus." Its basis was a communal-based asceticism of non-appropriation that represented "an alternative, non-violent, generous and wholehearted way of living in contrast to the greedy and lustful culture of his day," and, Crosby contends, of our own day, as well.

The power inherent in this form of asceticism is the subject of the remaining sections of Crosby's presentation. Crosby uses the work of Richard Valantis to establish that the asceticism of non-appropriation adopted by Francis does not simply reject other ways of living. Rather, it rejects them precisely in order to embrace another existence, a way of life that has the power to create a new person, restructure society, and revise the understanding of the universe. This power was exemplified in the social consequences of Francis's encounter with the lepers of Assisi: the creation of "an alternative community of right relationships (i.e. justice) based on non-appropriation, 'purity of heart,' and trust," which Francis called "the Gospel way of life."

In the final two sections of his presentation, Crosby considers Francis's understanding of what living the Gospel meant both for his lesser brothers and sisters personally and for their communal relationship to "the world." According to Crosby, Francis formed his threefold understanding in the light of Jesus' teaching that whoever does the will of his heavenly Father is his brother, sister, and mother: (1) withdrawal from traditional forms of belonging, (2) living as an alternative community of equals committed to the will of their "heavenly Father," and (3) taking up the cross as the consequence of the Gospel-way of justice. This Gospel way of life, this asceticism of non-appropriation had a profound impact upon Francis's world, as it can upon our world, if we embrace it with a pure heart as lesser brothers and sisters to people so affected by the abusive power of greed and lust that they can hardly imagine another way of life.

It is appropriate that the presentation by Professor Darleen Pryds, Ph.D., follows that by Crosby. In it, Pryds' research into the leadership exercised by laywomen in the nascent Franciscan Movement responds to the imperative Crosby identified above: the Franciscan vocation to live as an alternative community of equals. In the service of a first step, Pryds leads the way.

These forgotten women were among the most significant Franciscans of their day: Rose of Viterbo, an example of Franciscan evangelism; Angela of Foligno, a prominent teacher in the early Franciscan spiritual and theological tradition; Margaret of Cortona, the *Third Light* of the Franciscan Order; Sancia of Naples, protector and counselor of the Friars Minor. It is ironic that these women were so forgotten, given the value that Francis placed upon his own relationship with Lady Jacoba. Certainly, the possibility of scandal was present. Nevertheless, Pryds argues, the reason for this forgetfulness lay deeper, and is still present among members of the First and Second Orders: "the temptation of judging laity as fundamentally different in the seriousness of our spiritual commitments because of the difference in ecclesial status." Yet, Pryds contends, "a spirituality of mutuality… is one that our world and our Church desperately needs today. It is also one that Francis experimented with in his own life, and we would do well to explore more openly and honestly."

Pryds concludes her presentation by noting how our present "interpersonal problems and challenges for ministry" may find part of their solution in "the medieval Franciscan approach to ministry and faith formation forged by Francis and Jacoba, and implemented in the early generations of Franciscan life by Rose, Angela, Margaret and Sancia." When we forget the complexities of our historical tradition, it is easy, Pryds states, "to overlook the radical mutual engagement and equality that lay women and friars experienced and experimented with in the first century of the order. But returning to a mere recognition of such a tradition could be a wake up call to laity and clergy alike" within the Franciscan Family.

The work of building a more just world cannot fail to take account of the power exercised by cold hard cash. "It's the economy, stupid" is more than a political mantra today. It defines many of the real-world anxieties and fears of people today. Therefore, our Franciscan Symposium concludes with the presentation by Vincent DePaul Cushing, O.F.M., S.T.D., former president of the Washington Theological Union and chairman of the board of the Washington, DC based Center of Concern.

At the outset of his presentation, Cushing notes, "there is a sound foundation for saying there is a distinctly Franciscan approach to the economy and how we participate in it." Cushing develops this thesis in three parts: (1) he describes one example from Franciscan history that sheds light on how the Franciscan Tradition can shape our approach to the present economic situation, (2) he reflects on how contemporary papal teaching on the economy can serve the development of our approach, and (3) he offers conclusions "to help articulate our own spirituality in the face of the challenges to social justice in our day."

The historical example that Cushing describes is the *Montes Pietatis*: the credit unions of the Middle Ages which Franciscans established to protect people from usury. The *Montes Pietatis* witness three elements vital to any Franciscans foray into the present economic situation (1) an understanding of the economy, (2) an appreciation of its limitations, and (3) a commitment to practical solutions capable of helping those in need. Yet, sufficient knowledge of the situation is not enough if our approach is to be genuinely Franciscan, i.e., rooted in the Gospel. It also must have a "robust theological foundation." For this, Cushing turns to contemporary papal teaching on the economy, specifically the recent encyclical of Pope Benedict XVI, *Caritas in Veritate*.

As Cushing notes, it is the Kingdom of God that provides the strongest theological foundation for Franciscans' worldwide ministry of peace and justice, especially economic justice, and their surest guide as to the shape their ministry should take.

When turning to the practice of economic justice in our day, Cushing draws attention to one of the Franciscan Action Network's "white papers" on economic justice, in which David Couturier, O.F.M., Cap., Ph.D. directly addresses the economic dilemma that the US is currently experiencing. Couturier offers several basic guidelines for Franciscans: transparency, equity, participation, solidarity, and austerity. With these principles in mind, Cushing concludes that, in accord with the theological principle that orthopraxy precedes orthodoxy, a "'Franciscan economy' needs first to be realized within the Franciscan family itself."

In his *Testament*, Francis of Assisi tells us: "When I was in sin, it seemed too bitter for me to see lepers. And the Lord himself led me among them and I showed mercy to them. And when I left them, what had seemed bitter to me was turned into sweetness of soul and body. And afterwards I delayed a little and left the world (1-3)." In this brief passage we find most of the elements identified by the presenters of this year's Franciscan Symposium: conscientization, the asceticism of non-appropriation, and lived, effective solidarity with the most marginalized of people. Only one element remains: "And after the Lord gave me some brothers, no one showed me what I had to do, but the Most High Himself revealed to me that I should live after the pattern of the Holy Gospel (*Test.*, 14)."

A community of brothers and sisters, enlivened by the belief that they are a gift to one another and to the world from the Lord himself, is an essential characteristic, perhaps the *sine qua non* of Franciscan identity, and hence of every Franciscan strategy for building a more just world. It is this which makes Franciscans a truly counter-cultural community not only within the world, but within the Church as well. It reminds all Christians – not the least being Franciscans themselves – of what is entailed in their call to live the Gospel of our Lord Jesus Christ (cf. *LR*, 1): to follow in the footsteps of Jesus, the eschatological prophet of God's Kingdom and Messiah of those who "hunger and thirst for righteousness (Matt 5:6)." I do not believe a surer antidote to greed, lust and power can be found.

Russel Murray, O.F.M., Ph.D.
Assistant Professor of Systematic Theology
Coordinator of the 2010 Franciscan Symposium

Greed, Lust and Power: Franciscan Strategies for Building a More Just World: Three Disturbing Hypotheses

Joseph Nangle, O.F.M.

Introduction

Let me first say a word about hypotheses. By definition they are tentative, non-conclusive, or to use a popular neologism "guesstimates." The dictionary defines "hypothesis" as "an assertion subject to verification or proof ... a conjecture."

I say this at the outset of this reflection as a disclaimer – perhaps even an apology – for what I will say about the overall topic of our symposium this weekend: "Franciscan Strategies for Building a More Just World." The three hypotheses are observations I have made during what is by now a long and quite joyous life as a Franciscan. I make no particular claim to certainty regarding the validity of these statements. They are my own, quite fallible and absolutely open for discussion.

In fact, as I begin here, I feel somewhat like the promoters of many modern medicines. We've all seen how the advertising for these remedies often includes warnings about the possible serious or even lethal side effects they could cause – "you may experience palpitations," "fainting spells may occur," "in some cases fatal heart attacks could happen," "speak to your doctor before using this product." And don't we often react to these ads thinking that it would be much better not to try them at all?

In addition, some hypotheses are more probable or readily acceptable than others. My guess is that of the three which I offer here, the first may be less of a challenge than the second and third.

In any case here they are.

FIRST DISTURBING HYPOTHESIS

Power, Lust and Greed fairly well describe the American Empire of the twentieth and twenty-first centuries. All of us who have spent significant time living abroad and seen the United States through the lens of another people in another culture know how different our country looks from that perspective. That is one of the great benefits of overseas experience – being able to see our country of origin, our culture from quite another point of view.

My fifteen years of service in two of my province's Latin American missions brought me to an increasing awareness that the United States represents the latest example of world powers that have included Rome, Spain and Great Britain – to name just three – which have earned the name "empire" in the course of human history. Without going into too much detail on my time overseas, from the vantage point of Bolivia and Peru I came to see that the United States is the proverbial "500 pound gorilla" in today's family of nations. Our country has an economic, political, sociological and cultural projection that literally spans the globe and imposes itself on virtually every country on earth.

I saw first-hand this projection in action during my time in Peru when the government there quite legitimately attempted to nationalize an American-owned iron mine which had long-since yielded profits that far exceeded the company's initial investment. In the end Peru had to back down in the face of threats from our country to cut our foreign aid to them. That's an empire at work.

More recently, others have described the American Empire with even more precision. It is said that the US imposes its will on the whole planet, too often unconcerned with the consequences of its imperial reach. Thus, in terms of the subject matter for this

Symposium, imperial America exemplifies most of the effects of Greed, Lust and Power:

- it dictates economic policies through impositions such as NAFTA and CAFTA (the so-called "free trade agreements") and through its overbearing influence in lending institutions such as the World Bank and the International Monetary Fund
- it contributes inordinately to the destruction of the planet through excessive consumption (the well-known statistic: 6% of the world's population using 40% of its resources), through air pollution, and in recent decades our insatiable need for oil which has resulted in ecological disasters such as the one currently taking place in the Gulf of Mexico
- it has initiated cruel wars, for example, in Afghanistan and Iraq, with little concern for life and death (during just one day in Fallujah, Iraq – April 11, 2004: 500 Iraqis were killed by US fire, 157 women and 146 children)
- it manipulates information without concern for the truth – note our country's stated reason for invading Iraq in the fall and spring of 2002 and 2003, the bogus claim about weapons of mass destruction in that country
- it shows no concern for international law – consider the lack of due process at Guantanamo prison or US refusal to acknowledge the World Court
- it imposes on the rest of the world the primacy of the (American) individual and her or his enjoyment of life
- it considers itself the lord and master of time – 9/11/2001 is an important date; 9/11 in 1973 (when the brutal American-backed dictatorship of Augusto Pinochet in Chile came to power) is not an important date
- it controls space – some space is protected (upper-class neighborhoods); some is not (inner-city neighborhoods); it considers outer space an appropriate venue for promoting our "national defense"
- it defines happiness as being upwardly (economically) mobile … in the American mode

The charges against the American Empire go on and on. As citizens of this country we can react defensively and cite the many positive aspects of our nation and society – individual freedoms, democratic processes, a basic sense of fairness among our people, etc. But I believe that in and around and above those many wholesome features of our society, the description by Pope John Paul II and more recently Pope Benedict XVI of ours as a "culture of death" rings true. The popes were not speaking only of abortion when they made these statements. And they aptly describe what happens when Greed, Lust and Power so clearly define a country's ethos.

This hypothesis, this understanding of our nation as empire, I submit, is the ever-so-challenging framework within which we are called by God to build a more just world. We are the People of God in the Franciscan tradition at this historical moment and place; at the same time we are citizens of the American Empire, destined to live and practice our faith in what many across the planet call "the belly of the beast." We surely did not choose this here and now for ourselves; we may not even wish to be part of it. But the fact is that accepting the truth of this hypothesis, gives us no choice but to deal with this modern version of empire from our Christian and Franciscan traditions.

SECOND DISTURBING HYPOTHESIS

Franciscan scholars and Franciscan spirituality generally tend to face the past in addressing the present and the future. As I mentioned in the introduction, this observation may prove the most challenging for you, or perhaps even unacceptable. I remain entirely open to contrary opinions here. What is more, I readily admit that I am not in any sense of the word a scholar, only a pastoral practitioner.

However, it has been my experience over many years now that we Franciscans seem to take on present and future challenges by looking backward. It's as if we are driving a car, guided almost completely by what we can see in our rear view mirrors, or with our GPS units set for where we've been. Said another way, we often reach back in our history for clues as to how we might proceed today and tomorrow.

That is not to say that our history is in any way irrelevant, or that we should not refer to it. The well-known phrase "those who refuse to learn from history are condemned to repeat it," applies to us as much as to any other group of people. But my problem with Franciscan scholarship and to a great extent Franciscan spirituality is that we remain wedded to the experiences of our movement in its earliest stages, impressive as those were.

Two examples of what I am trying to say here. During my years in Bolivia one of our mission superiors was an older friar, who obviously loved the Order and its traditions. One evening several of us were sharing the unique experiences of ministry in that special country and someone mentioned the great work which Maryknoll missioners were doing there. After listening to several such comments, this older brother flatly stated: "Maryknoll has nothing to teach us; we've been in business for 800 years."

A second example: listening to one of our Franciscan scholars several years ago, I was surprised to hear him say that he not only loved the thirteenth century but, in fact, wished that he lived then.

As I reviewed several volumes of the Franciscan Heritage Series in preparation for this Symposium and a number of articles from various Franciscan spiritual journals, I detected the same mindset I see reflected in those two examples. I believe that our scholars and spiritual writers – all of us really – have to do a better job of "connecting the historical dots" between the rich and truly cutting edge tradition which is ours and twenty-first century American life as described in the first hypothesis.

I also have to confess in the interest of full disclosure that this hypothesis about looking through a rear view mirror to discern the future has been challenged. I have been told that especially our younger scholars, both women and men, are indeed connecting those dots in most creative ways; that they are allowing our history to illumine the present without getting bound up by that history. In fact, my connection with Franciscan Action Network – our Washington-based public policy office – offers a modern example of Franciscans squarely facing the present and the future. But my overall experience still suggests that by and large in the Franciscan family the tendency is to look more backward than forward, especially regarding current matters of urgency. So I present this hypothesis for your consideration and perhaps your action.

THIRD DISTURBING HYPOTHESIS

We must as much look outside of our Franciscan worldview as inside it to find strategies for building a more just world. Obviously, this statement follows directly from the previous hypothesis. It also stands on its own, apart from what has already been said. To effectively live out our Christian-Catholic-Franciscan convictions in the heart of the American Empire, we must employ much more than our admittedly rich Franciscan traditions to find our way.

Let me, therefore, cite three non-Franciscan resources which I consider essential for crafting strategies to create a more just world – to overcome the Greed, Lust and Power which surround us.

First, Catholic Social Teaching (CST). This "new grace" of the Holy Spirit for our times offers quite amazing insights and challenges for us who live and minister here in the American Empire. In my own life CST has quite frankly inspired me more than any Franciscan source when it comes to dealing with today's and tomorrow's global, national and ecclesial issues.

A recent example of CST, and its application to our realities comes from Pope Benedict XVI's Encyclical letter *Caritas in Veritate*, published last summer. Listen to these prescient words in light of the ecological disaster happening right now in the Gulf of Mexico:

> Entranced by an exclusive reliance on technology, reason without faith is doomed to flounder in an illusion of its own omnipotence…. In this type of culture, the conscience is simply invited to take note of technological possibilities … we must not underestimate the disturbing scenarios that threaten our future, or the powerful new instruments that the 'culture of death' has at its disposal (*Caritas in Veritate* 74-75).

Surely, Catholic Social Teaching has to become part of any Franciscan response to the signs of our times, to the Greed, Lust and Power which cry out for new strategies.

Second, the Social Sciences. Catholic Social Teaching has made extensive use of disciplines such as economics, sociology, political and physical sciences to analyze today's world and give us ever-so helpful frameworks in the pursuit of a more just world. Just the titles of a few great Catholic social documents demonstrate how much they lean on these secular resources. "On the Development of Peoples," "Human Work," "On the Reconstruction of the Social Order," "Justice in the World" and so many others – all point to the value of social sciences for judging how and why people of faith are called to struggle for Gospel/Kingdom values in the world of today and tomorrow. In addition, the aforementioned encyclical *Caritas in Veritate* of 2009 offers insights into relatively new problems such as globalization and ecological destruction.

Third, Social Analysis. Modern methods of Social Analysis stand as crucial strategies for building a more just world. These methods are actually quite simple and direct (observe, judge and act, the Circle of Praxis or Pablo Freire's teaching tool called "conscientization" – the last two developed in Latin America). They provide most useful processes for action plans aimed at overcoming Greed, Lust and Power, for moving toward a world of justice. So much more could be said about these methods, especially what happens when they are NOT employed.

For example, in the intentional community where I live we gather each morning for prayer. On our way into the living room for our half-hour of biblical reflection and sharing, each of us glances at the New York Times and the Washington Post lying on our dining room table. That quick scan of the events of our world, nation and neighborhood inevitably informs our prayer together. That's Social Analysis, something we have found invaluable, not to say essential, for our prayer time.

On the other hand some work I do with American vowed religious has brought me to the realization that we do not readily make use of Social Analysis on a regular basis. It does not seem to form part of our "DNA" the way it does among religious and laity in Latin America. This blind spot strikes me as most unfortunate, and perhaps a principal reason for the drift in American religious life today.

CONCLUSION – A STORY

I wish to conclude with a personal anecdote. During my years in Peru I had the immense good fortune to learn from and collaborate closely with the leadership of that church – bishops, theologians, pastoral agents and committed laity – who were most actively engaged in social justice ministries. Years later I heard that I was considered an "atypical" Franciscan, meaning that it was most unusual for someone affiliated to our family to be found in that progressive company.

That strikes me as sad and extremely unfortunate. With our history, and its amazing story of Francis and Clare, together with all the other early Franciscan giants, we have the motivation and the mystique to translate our charism into a real contribution to all the wonderful work being done today on behalf of Justice, Peace and the Integrity of Creation. But, as my major thesis today would have it: we must bring that tradition to bear on today's and tomorrow's challenges by knowing what they are and joining with all others of good will in dealing with them.

FRANCIS OF ASSISI'S STRATEGIC INSIGHT ABOUT POWER IN A WORLD OF GREED AND LUST: A MODEL [OF ASCETICISM] FOR EVERY AGE

MICHAEL H. CROSBY, O.F.M. CAP.

When I was told the overall theme for our days together was "greed" and "lust" from the perspective of power I thought such a topic might be better developed as an episode on Desperate Housewives than a symposium at WTU. However, as I watched these very same dynamics played out in the ongoing passion play found in the pedophilia scandals plaguing our church's hierarchy, I thought I might probe their connection as the topic of my paper. However, already having written on this subject[1] and having just finished Joe Chinnici's newly-published book,[2] I don't think my "two cents" stressing the need for community as an antidote to this sinful situation would be all that new.

I also knew if I developed this idea, I'd likely be pointing fingers. Knowing any finger pointed at others has four pointed back, I decided to change my direction. This was reinforced by Francis's advice in the *Early Rule*. Instead of considering others' "least sins," we should "reflect more upon" our "own sins in the bitterness of" our souls (ER 11:11-12; see ER 22:7). I also recall Bonaventure's words in his *Collations on the Ten Commandments*:

---

[1] Michael H. Crosby, *The Dysfunctional Church: Addiction and Codependency in the Family of Catholicism* (Notre Dame, IN: Ave Maria Press, 1991). Michael H. Crosby, *Rethinking Celibacy, Reclaiming the Church* (Eugene, OR: Wipf and Stock, 2003).

[2] Joseph P. Chinnici, *When Values Collide: The Catholic Church, Sexual Abuse, and the Challenges of Leadership* (Maryknoll, NY: Orbis, 2010). Hereafter cited as Chinnici.

All incorrect evaluations of creatures come either from a
sense of high-mindedness, or from the desire for sufficien-
cy, or from pleasure. The first way is the idolatry of the
proud, the second way is the idolatry of the greedy, and the
third way is the idolatry of the lascivious.[3]

When I considered Francis's point in the *Early Rule* that the
only thing we can know with certainty is that "nothing belongs
to us except our vices and sins" (ER 17:7), I discovered the core
insight that will guide my remarks this evening. Realizing that the
only thing that "belongs to us" (or which we have appropriated
to ourselves) are our own vices and sins (such as lust and greed)
I summarize my remarks for this evening in the following thesis:
the vices and sins of lust and greed are the result of appropriating
something good (i.e. sexuality and wealth) in ways that represent
an abuse not only of power but of relationships that create authentic community. As a result only an individual and communal stance
of non-appropriation, "purity of heart" and trusting relationships
will serve as an antidote to their controlling power.

THE INTERCONNECTEDNESS OF LUST AND GREED WITH POWER

The more I consider the three notions of lust, power and
greed, I find their negative expressions writ large in many parts of
our institutional church and culture. As I already have indicated
why I won't discuss their manifestation in the institutional church
I will develop here how the three can be found in our culture and
how this demands prophetic communities of justice that witness
to an alternative, observable way of organizing our relationships.
In this effort I am buttressed by three authors (besides myself, I
guess I'd have to add[4]) who call for mediating institutions to bring

---

[3] St. Bonaventure, *Collations on the Ten Commandments*, Works of St. Bonaventure VI, introduction and translation by Paul J. Spaeth (St. Bonaventure,
NY: The Franciscan Institute, 1996), II.29, 42-43.

[4] I first developed the need for alternative communities of conscientization
and conversion within the infrastructure of institutions, "isms" [i.e., unequal power relationships] and their accompanying ideology in Michael H. Crosby, O.F.M.

balance and a sense of community to our increasingly fractured culture: Robert Bellah and his *Habits of the Heart: Individualism and Commitment in American Life*;[5] Wendell Berry in his various writings, especially his essay on "Sex, Economy, Freedom & Community," and, just recently, Joe Chinnici in his *When Values Collide: The Catholic Church, Sexual Abuse, and the Challenges of Leadership*.

To summarize their thoughts, Bellah et als' thesis is that, because individualism is at the heart of the culture and reinforced in our economics, politics and entertainment, committed relationships are undermined. Therefore we need what they call "Communities of Memory" to serve as mediating institutions of meaning.[6] Joe Chinnici argues in much the same way. Because disordered affections drive relational power in the Church and other parts of the "social body," there is a need for what he calls the mediating institution of "Fraternity-in-Mission" that is "ascetically exacting."[7]

Notwithstanding the insights of Bellah and the pertinence of Chinnici to our topic, I would argue that few have done a better job of making such a clear link between greed and lust with power as Wendell Berry, especially in one essay in his *Sex, Economy, Freedom and Community: Eight Essays*. This particular essay, as well as many of his other writings, represents a powerful examination of the commercialism, promiscuity and unfettered ambition and power that is undermining the dignity of human beings and the possibility of community in private and public life. His argument can be summarized in one key sentence: "The indispensable form that can intervene between public and private interests is that of community." He explains further:

Cap., *Thy Will Be Done: Praying the Our Father as Subversive Activity* (Maryknoll, NY: Orbis, 1977), esp. 163-211. I moved my social analysis from a tri-level approach (individual, interpersonal and infrastructural) to include the fourth level of the ecological (including the environmental) in the second edition of my *Spirituality of the Beatitudes: Matthew's Vision for the Church in an Unjust World* (Maryknoll, NY: Orbis, 2005).

[5] Robert N. Bellah, Richard Madsen, William M. Sullivan, Ann Swidler, and Steven M. Tipton, *Habits of the Heart: Individualism and Commitment in American Life* (Berkeley, CA: University of California Press, 1985).

[6] Bellah, et al., especially 152-63.

[7] Chinnici, 130, see also 91-94, passim.

Community alone, as principle and as fact, can raise the standards of local health (ecological, economic, social, and spiritual) without which the other two interests will destroy one another.[8]

I will also argue that, in the budding stages of the seminal, emerging capitalistic relationships of his day, Francis's strategic insight about power was surprisingly nuanced. Negatively he saw power in the form of abuse or control as a manifestation of violence. This violence undermined persons as well as community, especially communal relationships of trust. In a gift economy mutuality was more assured; now that the gift economy was being replaced by a money-based economic order, he saw the traditional ways of human exchange undermined. When this power was associated with property he concluded that claims related to property were the source of all divisions, conflicts and violence among humans; thus he would embrace non-appropriation. This got expressed more positively in the way he saw his fraternity as one wherein all members would make no claims on each other but would rather "confidently make known to each other" and the wider society their needs in a way that would not make them or others dependent on money, a key source of the vices and sins of concupiscence represented in greed and lust or covetousness which he saw as arising from disordered affections of the heart (ER 22:7-8; see ER 12:5 and 1Frg, 32; LR 10; Adm 27:3).

Echoing Francis, Wendell Berry sees that the triumph of late industrialized capitalism has been accompanied by the collapse of community, including something else Francis did not discuss: sexual intimacy. For him the power of sex is harnessed in marriage when two people join in "the freedom of sexual consent and into the fullest earthly realization of the image of God."[9] However this sexual form of power also has its shadow side: in the way its abuse "has forsaken trust" because "it rests on the easy giving and breaking of promises."[10] As commitments and community deterio-

---

[8] Wendell Berry, "Sex, Economy, Freedom & Community," in *Sex, Economy, Freedom & Community: Eight Essays* (New York and San Francisco: Pantheon Books, 1993), 119. Hereafter cited as Berry.

[9] Berry, 138.

[10] Berry, 139.

rate, even the public language about sexuality comes "under the influence of private lust, ambition, and greed."[11] So, in this quote from Berry, you find all three notions we'll be discussing brought together in a powerful indictment regarding the "sin" of our particular culture.

Although Berry almost equates the three terms, I will argue that "greed," "lust," and "power" are not parallel notions. In the two places where the word for "greed" appears in the gospels (Mark 7:22; Luke 12:15), it is negative. However, lust is another matter. If we look at *epithymia* in the gospels, it is seen differently: 1) as negative (John 8:44; see James 1:14; 2 Peter 1:4); 2) positive in the sense of longing (Luke 22:15) and 3) neutral as a kind of desire for others or things (Mark 4:19).[12] Aware of this, and while some may offer different theoretical nuances regarding where the three words may have similarities and dissimilarities, in common parlance, where we limit ourselves to words and notions surrounding "greed" and "lust," I follow the general norm of finding them negative. Thus Gregory the Great listed them among the seven sins that he considered to be "capital" or caput. In his mind they represented negative dynamics controlling the affections at the center of life.

Despite what Gordon Gekko said about greed,[13] neither it nor lust are "good." Whether manifested personally, communally or collectively, they are deadly. They kill relationships; represent disordered affections and desires and, for this reason, have always been called "deadly sins." Spirituality is the response we make to their power in our lives so that, rather than being defined by these deadly forces we might have a genuine quality of life. Such spiritu-

---

[11] Berry, 122.

[12] Despite its appearance outside the gospels, there are only two places where the word for greed appears in the gospels. *Pleonezia* appears as a negative notion in Mark 7:22 and Luke 12:15. *Epithymia* is more nuanced in the gospels. It appears as a neutral term in Mark 4:19, in a positive sense in Luke 22:15 and in a negative sense of desiring something forbidden or foolish in John 8:44. In its verb form, *epithymia*, it appears most often as a positive (as longing or desire) in Matt 13:17 and Luke 15:16; 16:21; 17:22; 22:15) and only once negatively in the form of "lust" (Matt 5:28).

[13] Gordon Gekko is to return in Fall, 2010 in an Oliver Stone sequel to his 1987 movie, *Wall Street: Money Never Sleeps*. For a preview, see Liam Lacy, "Gekko's Glitzy Greed Returns—with Cancon," *The Globe and Mail*, May 15, 2010, R5.

ality, Tom Cahil has written in his article "The Deadly Sins, Alive and Well,"

> enables us to face and deal with evil and sin, deadly or oth-
> erwise, in ourselves and in society. So when a deadly sin
> rears its ugly head spirituality spurs us to counteract it.[14]

With these initial reflections on greed and lust, as we discuss "power," we find its meaning much more ambiguous. As I have shown elsewhere,[15] if power is defined as "the ability to influence," then it is a neutral concept. It all depends on how that power is exercised in our personal, communal and organizational living. Whether we consider power scientifically as a form of energy or force as biblically as the reign, rule or governance of the Trinitarian God, we know that such expressions of power do not take place isolated from other forms of power. So, while power can be good or not good; all things considered, greed and lust are never good. Lust and greed involve disordered desires; power can arise from desire that is ordered or disordered, selfish or altruistic.

Before moving to more thoughts about Francis's "Strategic Insight" or approach to power that offered an alternative to his culture of violence marked by greed and lust, I'd like to suggest that, if greed and lust are identified with sin, then any strategic insight to address them that arose from Francis would have to involve some kind of asceticism or discipline; such would offer an alternative to their power over peoples' lives and relationships. This is indicated in the opening lines of his Testament. He made a link among being "in sin," "being in the world" and his encounter with the leper and the change that came to him "in soul and body" when he changed his way of relating to the leper; this changed the way he would be part of sin and part of "the world."

When we go deeper into the three themes of this conference we see them embodied in the reality and metaphor of the "leper."

---

[14] Tom Cahil, S.V.D., "The Deadly Sins, Alive and Well," *Spirituality* 15, no. 83 (2009): 119.

[15] Michael H. Crosby, *The Paradox of Power: From Control to Compassion* (New York: Crossroad Publishing Company, 2008). See also the parallel DVD series, *Choosing Compassion: The Paradox of Power*. For more information see www.choosingcompassion.net.

Not only did the reality and notion of the "leper" define definite boundary-markers around purity and group (non)identification in ways outlined by Mary Douglas.[16] They also personified the lack of power. Even more, on them were projected all the fears people had regarding their own vices. In his new book, Joe Chinnici writes of them:

> Physically disfigured, they were also [perceived as] individuals full of unruly emotional disorders: anger, craftiness, sexual lust, greed, deception, perversion, manipulation, evil intentions.[17]

Their disfigurement embodied the lack of power and absence of the ability to participate in community. Not only were they "poor in health," they were considered "poor in virtue, poor in resources. The deformity of leprosy represented a threat to a stable and prosperous" order, including community.[18]

When Francis talked about the time in his life when he was "still in sin" and the time, after his embrace of the leper, that found him "leaving the world" his non-appropriation of these forms of vice, including greed and lust, represented another way of using power. He called this way of discipleship "walking in the footprints of Jesus." His communal based, non-appropriation of a property-defined way of life represented an alternative, non-violent, generous and wholehearted way of living in contrast to the greedy and lustful culture of his day.

Furthermore, because, unlike Francis's understanding of the debilitating power of greed, we do not find much, if anything, related to the traditional notion of lust as having to do with sex and reproduction, in his actual writings, I am going to interpret "lust" as having to do with covetousness – not ala the ninth commandment vis-à-vis the neighbor's spouse but the tenth commandment about not coveting or lusting after or being obsessed with getting the neighbor's goods. Whether greed or lust, I will argue, both are forms of appropriation that must be addressed negatively through

---

[16] Mary Douglas, *Purity and Danger: An Analysis of the Concepts of Pollution and Taboo* (London: Routledge, 1991).

[17] Chinnici, 168-69.

[18] Chinnici, 168-69.

expropriation and positively through purity of heart. Above all, these must be done in a community of disciples called brothers and sisters who are defined by trust and solidarity. In contrast to the vices of greed and lust, we manifest a new communal model of asceticism that offers a creative antidote to the addictive power of greed and lust. This is done in community through what Joe Chinnici calls an "ascetical ethic."[19]

ASCETICISM AS AN ALTERNATIVE POWER IN RESPONSE TO THE PRESENCE OF GREED AND LUST

Arguably one of the most clear and helpful attempts articulating a kind of meta-theory of asceticism can be found in Richard Valantis's 1995 piece in the *Journal of the American Academy of Religion* entitled: "Constructions of Power in Asceticism." According to him, asceticism involves "performances within a dominant social environment intended to inaugurate a new subjectivity, different social relations, and an alternative symbolic universe."[20] Valantis's definition of asceticism, within a dominant social environment (for us "greed" and "lust" of Francis's day and ours) involves what he calls "performances" that inaugurate something quite alternative. This occurs in three key modes of being: 1) a new way of relating in society; 2) that witnesses to a counter-cultural way of life; and 3) through concrete symbolic forms.

I think it is key here to consider two points made by Valantis in his definition regarding the first two components of his triad: it involves not just something that is personal or a "new subjectivity"; it is this very subjectivity that becomes contagious to those contaminated by the "sin of the world," in our case "greed" and "lust." This involves the creation of "different social relations" that stand over-and-against the prevailing "symbolic universe." He declares:

Asceticism does not simply reject other ways of living (that is the misconception denoted by the negative implications

---

[19] Chinnici, 102, 130.
[20] Richard Valantis, "Constructions of Power in Asceticism," *Journal of the American Academy of Religion* 63 (1995): 797.

of the word "asceticism"), but rather asceticism rejects precisely in order to embrace another existence, another way of living embodied in a new subjectivity, alternative social relations, and a new imaging of the universe. And this intentionality has power—power to create a new person, power to restructure society, power to revise the understanding of the universe.[21]

I find it fascinating that, just after Francis articulates in his Testament how he inaugurated his conversion with the leper-experience, he immediately notes that "the Lord gave me brothers." In other words, his personal conversion represents a strategic and symbolic use of power that had social consequences or impact. Whether or not this was a conscious "strategy" or not is not important here. The fact was that, in the coming together of the first friars, poor women and seculars, a powerful association of men and women came to embody what Peter Berger and Thomas Luckmann call an alternative "Social Construction of Reality."[22] This Francis called the "gospel way of life."

Building on these thoughts, I'd like to spend the rest of my paper developing three themes: 1) evangelical asceticism in the New Testament; 2) Francis's way of "withdrawal" from the world of lust and greed in the form of "non-appropriation"; and 3) the creation of an alternative community of right relationships (i.e. justice) based on non-appropriation, "purity of heart," and trust.

EVANGELICAL ASCETICISM IN THE NEW TESTAMENT

As I begin my remarks about "evangelical asceticism in the New Testament," I want to acknowledge my indebtedness to two key sources. I've already mentioned *Asceticism and the New Testament*.[23] The second comes from one of the editors of the first source, Leif E. Vaage. It's his "An Other Home: Discipleship in

---

[21] Valantis, 799.
[22] Peter L. Berger and Thomas Luckmann, *The Social Construction of Reality: A Treatise in the Sociology of Knowledge* (Garden City, NY: Doubleday, 1966).
[23] Leif E. Vaage and Vincent L. Wimbush, eds., *Asceticism and the New Testament* (New York and London: Routledge, 1999).

Mark as Domestic Asceticism"[24] in a recent issue of the *Catholic Biblical Quarterly*.

When I consider their approach to asceticism and Chinnici's notion of brotherhood/sisterhood being an expression of "ethical asceticism," I find both echoing Wendell Berry's insight about the power of community being the antidote to greed and lust. I find in the Synoptic Gospels insights about evangelical asceticism as linked to a special kind of communal discipline or discipleship which Francis called "walking in the footprints of our Lord Jesus Christ." This begins in a "withdrawal" from one metaphorical way of life or "doing business" to embrace an alternative community, family or business model.[25]

While it is clear that the evangelical model of asceticism cannot be equated with the classical understanding and patterns of asceticism that originated from the Greek notion and practice of *askein* (which originally referred to physical discipline and later morphed into including moral and/or personal training or discipline), there are two core elements from the Greek form that can be found in the asceticism of the evangelical way: a withdrawal from the main cultural patterns and dynamics accompanied by the creation of alternative expressions that would be considered "counter-cultural." The Synoptic Gospels articulate this asceticism as the "leaving of everything" for the embrace of discipleship.[26] Francis expressed it as the gospel way of life that involved "leaving the world" [of "sin"] in order to "walk in the footprints of our Lord Jesus Christ."

Sharon Daloz Parks brings these two notions together in her contention that, what I call "withdrawal" and "community" or fraternity, represent the two key organizational metaphors for life itself. She writes:

[24] Leif E. Vaage, "An Other Home: Discipleship in Mark as Domestic Asceticism," *Catholic Biblical Quarterly* 71: 741-61.

[25] I highly recommend an article that shows that "withdrawal" and "community" represent core metaphors for life itself, including the ascetical life: Sharon Daloz Parks, "Home and Pilgrimage: Companion Metaphors for Personal and Social Transformation," *Soundings* 72.2-3 (1989): 297-315.

[26] Tom Beaudoin discusses this connection between discipleship and asceticism in his *Witness to Dispossession: The Vocation of a Post-Modern Theologian* (Maryknoll, NY: Orbis, 2008), esp. 144-47.

A theory of faith development must ... be attentive to the transcendent and covenantal images and symbols—the deep, culturally confirmed metaphors by which meaning is given form and upon which moral-ethical being and becoming depends.

At this pivotal, dangerous, and promising moment in history, the formation of adequate forms of meaning and faith—and perhaps the future of our small planet home— is dependent, in part, upon the liberation, reappropriation, and renewed companionship of the metaphors of detachment and connection, pilgrims and homemakers, journeying and homesteading.[27]

When I consider the use of Matthew 12:46-50 in Francis's writings, especially in his Letters to the Faithful, I see his understanding of this asceticism as involving at least three clear patterns found in Matthew's wider gospel: 1) a withdrawal from traditional forms of patriarchal, familial notions of "belonging" or "doing business"; 2) the inauguration of an alternative model of family / economy /business that is not "business as usual" but rather the creation of a family or community of persons united with Jesus as equals insofar as they all lived under the household of the one called the "heavenly Father"; 3) and finally, the stress on the cross not only as an alternative to the greed and lust arising from issues dealing with power, possessions and prestige to which the "world" is addicted or "given over to" (*douleuein* [Matt 6:24]), but a sign of self-sacrificing love.

In his article on Mark, Leif Vaage calls this way of life "a form of domestic asceticism."[28] He writes:

In describing the depiction of successful discipleship in Mark as domestic asceticism, I reflect the fact that the

---

[27] Sharon Daloz Parks, "Home and Pilgrimage: Companion Metaphors for Personal and Social Transformation," *Listening* 72.2-3 (1989): 299, 301.

[28] Vaage, "An Other Home," 741. I refer to "house" as the "assumed primary metaphor" in Matthew's Gospel as the context for the whole Gospel. Michael H. Crosby, *Church, Economics and Justice in Matthew* (Eugene, OR: Wipf and Stock, 1988 [2004]), 10-15.

household is here the site where the otherwise 'anti-(conventional) family' and 'unfamiliar' habits of discipleship are supposed to be practiced. I also mean to suggest something else. I take the phrase 'domestic asceticism' from Patrick Olivelle's discussion of the history of Brahmanism, in which Olivelle has demonstrated how older Vedic forms of religion came to incorporate (and thereby to co-opt) the challenge to the traditional social order(s) of the Indian Subcontinent, which the more radically world-denying asceticisms of early Buddhism and Jainism embodied ...

At the same time, the asceticism of Mark is "domestic" ... Indeed, what makes it so is precisely Mark's conviction that the proper and most effective way to enter the kingdom of God is by redoing life at home.

Vaage concludes with words that are important for us Franciscans to hear: "This may be the evangelist's most enduring challenge to us."[29]

Building on Mark's insights as adapted by Matthew, let's now consider the First Gospel's approach to the ascetical life as the discipline of domestic (fraternal) asceticism.

1) *Leaving the traditional, patriarchal ways of "doing business."*

In Mark and Matthew we discover Jesus inaugurating what we may call "a new business model" for his disciples. After the infancy narrative Matthew echoes the pattern of Mark. Jesus embraces John the Baptist's way of life, beginning with a 40-day novitiate. When he hears that John has been arrested, Matthew tells us that Jesus "withdrew."

The notion of "withdrawal" *anachoresis* is at the heart of all forms of asceticism. While Mark uses the verb form only once (3:7), Matthew uses it seven times with four of these involving a Matthean triad of violence leading to withdrawal that finds the scriptures being fulfilled. In other words, only when one withdraws from violence in such forms as rape and lust of people or the planet or greed and avarice for more and more wealth, can

---

[29] Vaage, 744.

God's evangelical economy or project or will be accomplished in our life, since God's ways can never be found in the ways and forms of violence.

Having withdrawn, in order to have the Scripture fulfilled in him, Jesus wraps himself in the mantle of proclaiming the gospel of the kingdom/kindom of God. He inaugurates his ministry by calling for a change in his hearers' basic life stance: "Repent for the kingdom/ kindom of God ["heaven" in Matthew] is at hand."

Immediately after this he implements his business model by requiring a break from the traditional family business model defined by patriarchy and, in this case, expressed in the business of fishing. Vaage spells it out quite clearly:

> Thus, the first thing Jesus does ... is to break up a couple of family businesses by calling Peter and Andrew, then James and John, to follow him. The four men immediately abandon their parental household, leaving, the second instance, the sorry sight of their father alone in the boat with the hired help. This figure of parental abandonment is as important a feature of the first call narrative in Mark [and Matthew] as are the other elements.[30]

At the time of Jesus and the writing of Matthew's gospel, the household, the family, the business defined a certain kind of group-belonging around power relationships centered in the figure of the *pater familias*. When James and John leave their father and the boats, this signals the inauguration of a new kind of economy.

2) Embracing and witnessing to an alternative community of mothers/brothers/sisters (i.e., equals) committed to the business, the project, the will of the one called the "heavenly Father."

It is clear from all the Synoptics that the call to create a new way of doing business on earth as it is transacted in heaven never has any of the disciples, despite some proof-texting, ever leaving "everything." They always have a house to return to. However their home-making or way of doing business is, even then, defined

---

[30] Vaage, 746-47.

by Jesus' proclamation of the reign of the Family Business which
he came to inaugurate on earth as it was/is in heaven. Building on
Valantis's description of asceticism, Anthony J. Saldarini writes:

> Forced to choose, Matthew and his associates must go with
> their own group and not with their families, parents, or
> anyone who will impede their relationship with the teacher
> and master, Jesus. In this they stand against the powerful
> Near Eastern cultural assumption that one's family and
> kinship group come first. Matthew seeks to create a new
> personal and communal subjectivity with altered relation-
> ships not only to families but to society at large. Leaving
> home changes the fundamental structures of political and
> familial society with economic, religious, and cultural con-
> sequences for all.[31]

In my writings on the way the author of Matthew's Gospel developed the metaphor of "house" in the First Gospel, I show that
Jesus' form of discipleship demanded the creation of an alternative
familial-based community wherein all would be seen as brothers,
sisters and mothers under the one the author called "the heavenly
Father."[32]

If we structure Matthew's gospel as having a beginning (the
genealogy and infancy narrative) and end (the passion, death, and
resurrection narrative) within which we find the "five books," each
with a narrative and discourse, everything in the gospel builds to
and flows from Matthew 12:46-50.

Not only does Matthew 12:46-50 represent the pivot of the
gospel, it is clear from the two key changes the author makes from
the Markan source, that it is precisely Jesus' disciples who are different from the mainstream political economy precisely in the way
they become sisters, brothers and mothers or equals in a way that

---

[31] Anthony J. Saldarini, "Asceticism and the Gospel of Matthew," in Vaage
and Wimbush, *Asceticism and the New Testament*, 20. For another aspect of the
"asceticism" in Matthew's gospel, see J. Duncan M. Derrett, *The Ascetic Discourse:
An Explanation of the Sermon on the Mount* (Elisbrunn: Ko'amar, 1989).

[32] My doctoral dissertation on "house" in Matthew is found in Michael H.
Crosby, *House of Disciples: Church, Justice and Economics in Matthew* (Eugene, OR:
Wipf and Stock, 2002).

constitutes a new family ordering or business under the one called the heavenly [not earthly] father.

3) The parallel call to "take up the cross" as accepting suffering as the consequence of embarking on the way of justice as described in NN. 1 and 2.

In Matthew's Gospel it is very clear that the consequence of "withdrawing" from the "sin of the world," including greed or lust, especially from the abuse of power in entrenched religious entities and political economies like the Roman empire will result in persecution. The asceticism that is expressed in this way of life does not revolve around a whole set of specifics that deal with concrete forms of specific expressions of justice such as fasting, prayer and almsgiving but rather an underlying commitment to justice itself (Matt 6:1-16).

Thus, in Matthew's understanding of discipleship, the commitment to justice is what sets apart the disciple of Jesus; this is the discipline that is demanded of those who "withdraw" in order to have the scriptures fulfilled in them. In his article on "Asceticism and the Gospel of Matthew," Anthony Saldarini highlights this justice as Matthew's unique understanding of the asceticism or discipline of domestic discipleship very clearly. He notes that, while the "mastery of oneself through control of the passions is a major concern of Greek and Roman [ascetical] philosophy and ethical literature," Matthew's asceticism for his householders is defined by justice:

> Matthew understands righteousness or justice *dikaiosyne* to be "the right conduct which God requires." These just behaviors, including the attitudes and goals that are integral to them, demand a type of asceticism of the mind and body. Thus human behavior and society in Matthew are based on justice, just as in the Hebrew Bible and in Greek literature.... Matthew does not schematize these Greek reflections or use the same terms, but righteousness is deter-

mined for Matthew by inner attitudes and corresponding behaviors (5:20-6:18).[33]

Finally, referring to the notion of embracing the asceticism of the cross through persecution Saldarini concludes: "Inevitably, control of the passions becomes associated with Jesus' overcoming the most basic passion, the desire for life. In summary, hunger for justice (5:6) and seeking the justice of God's kingdom (6:33) require a behavior and personal formation that may be called ascetic."[34]

HOW FRANCIS'S APPROACH TO POWER VIA NON-APPROPRIATION AND COMMUNITY SERVED AS A CHALLENGE TO THE GREED AND LUST OF HIS DAY

Francis's conversion offered a non-violent power-alternative to greed and the violence which resulted from its abuse. This began with his own "withdrawal" from the world of violence in Apulia in order to have God's will fulfilled in him. This triad laid the foundation for everything else that would lead to his embrace of the gospel itself as the form of his future life and that of the first members of his new communal approach to the asceticism of "walking in the footsteps" of Jesus Christ. Even when he seriously violated in his own life and relationships with the brothers the triad of violence/withdrawal/scriptural fulfillment as in his "Great Temptation," I argue elsewhere, that, despite his negative form of "withdrawal," his openness to God's Word, enabled him to move beyond his violence toward the brothers and find the Scriptures fulfilled in him.[35]

At their core, both greed and lust undermine human relationships and community insofar as they treat human beings as objects rather than subjects. They create "I/It" relationships that abuse power through coercion, manipulation, exploitation or outright domination rather than "I/Thou" relationships that create a new kind of community based on trusting relationships of mutual soli-

---

[33] Saldarini, 23.

[34] Saldarini, 23-24.

[35] Michael H. Crosby, *Finding Francis, Following Christ* (Maryknoll, NY: Orbis, 2007).

darity. When the "other" becomes an object rather than a subject, that one becomes a source of acquisition and proprietorship; we want to control the other.

Francis came to understand that his "withdrawal" from that way of acquisitiveness and appropriation had to be realized by rejecting any form of proprietorship. Furthermore, since the vices of greed and lust represent disordered affections of the heart, the only way they could be countered, besides non-appropriation, would be by the cultivation of what he called "purity of heart" and the creation of trusting relationships among the brothers. It might be said that, for Francis, trust was the antidote of lust.

Now, recalling the three points which outlined "evangelical asceticism," let's see how Francis appropriated these notions in his personal life and offered them to his followers as a way of walking in the footprints of our Lord Jesus Christ.

1) *Leaving the traditional, patriarchal ways of "doing business."*

When I consider the scene in the Bishop's Palace of Francis, his Father and Guido, I think Franciscan scholarship has been remiss in sufficiently developing its meaning. I find in Francis's dispossession the move from one way of doing business or "making family" and the embrace of another. It involves a non-appropriation of the patriarchal capitalistic model of his abusive Father which was accompanied by the first steps toward an alternative way of living. The first part of this dynamic represented a "withdrawal" from the Bernadone Business model. When Francis declared he would henceforth say only "Our Father who art in heaven," we have his initial steps into another economic model wherein all members of the family would become nurtured by his motherly love as brothers and sisters. His gradual embrace of this alternative model of an oikonomia would not be defined by patriarchal hierarchy and clericalism and the forms of violence that are associated with their abuse (which make many greedy and lustful) but the embrace of a nurturing, more maternal form of inclusive community.

Ultimately, if George Lakoff, the "father" of framing is correct, we all live out of one of two main models of organizing our world with its accompanying "worldview." The first is the strict father image; the second is the nurturing parent model.[36] I am convinced that in the story of Francis's dispossession before Bishop Guido, he was withdrawing from one model to embrace a new asceticism of evangelical discipleship. This brings us to the second point about the evangelical way of life as shown in Francis's life and writings.

It was not only in Francis's insistence that we not use the terms "abbot" or "father" but servant and brother/sister that we see the alternative community being expressed. Especially in the First and Second Letters to the Faithful, Francis quotes the Matthean text above (Matt 12:46-50) about Jesus' new family of brothers, sisters and mothers; indeed he goes even further and waxes creatively on the new family dynamics of intimacy that are to be involved as well. Thus we read in the opening paragraphs of the Earlier Exhortation to the Brothers and Sisters of Penance:

> All those who love the Lord with their whole heart, with their whole soul and mind, with their whole strength and love their neighbors as themselves, who hate their bodies with their vices and sins, who receive the Body and Blood of our Lord Jesus Christ, and who produce worthy fruits of penance. O how happy and blessed are these men and women while they do such things and persevere in doing them, because the Spirit of the Lord will rest upon them and make Its home and dwelling place among them, and they are children of the heavenly Father whose works they do, and they are spouses, brothers, and mothers of our lord Jesus Christ.
>
> We are spouses when the faithful soul is joined by the Holy Spirit to our Lord Jesus Christ. We are brothers to him when we do the will of the Father who is in heaven. We are mothers when we carry him in our heart and body through a divine love and a pure and sincere conscience and give birth to him through a holy activity which must shine as an example before others (1LtF 1-10; 2 LtF, 48-53).[37]

---

[36] George Lakoff, *Don't Think of an Elephant!: Know Your Values and Frame the Debate—The Essential Guide for Progressives* (White River Jct., VT: Chelsea Green Publishing, 2004).
[37] *FA:ED* 1, 41-42, 48-49.

Such insights, Menestò writes,

> contain all of the mystical Francis, all of his Christ-cen-
> teredness 'which sees here the entire life of believers in
> terms of their relationship with the Father' and which opens
> 'seamlessly to a relationship with the entire Trinity.'[38]

In his effort to withdraw from the greed and lust involved in appropriating people and property to ourselves, Francis realized that such vices could only be overcome by a community wherein the familial dynamics of mothering trust define the relationships: "if a mother loves and cherishes her son/s according to the flesh, how much more are we to care for each other." The result should be the ability for us to create relational dynamics of trust: of "confidently" or trustingly making known our most basic needs.

We all need wealth in the form of basic power, possessions and prestige; it's when these core human needs are overcome by inordinate desires that they become vices such as greed, lust and other forms of covetousness or possessiveness. Only trust can break the addiction that these disordered affections express. Only when a new way of relating replaces the old can there be a new kind of communal ascetic. Joe Chinnici says it well when he declares that "relational power permeates and shapes all other uses of power. If the affections are not ordered toward relationality and trust, power in its manifest expressions can become destructive of community"[39] through such vices as greed and lust.

2) *Embracing and witnessing to an alternative community of mothers/brothers/sisters (i.e., equals) committed to the business, the project, the will of the one called the "heavenly Father."*

In this section I want to highlight the critical, counter-cultural stance of non-appropriation which Francis embraced. Among its various manifestations, I want to highlight the deeply personal element of it around "non-appropriation" vis-à-vis the notion of

---

[38] Enrico Menestò, quoting C. Paolazzi, "Lettura degli scriti di Francesco d'Assisi," (Milan, 1987), 158, in "A Re-reading of Francis of Assisi's Letter To The Faithful," *Greyfriars Review* 14.2 (2000): 107.

[39] Chinnici, 93.

"rights," and the deeply structural notion of using non-appropriation as a non-violent way of undermining the "proprietorship" that is at the heart of all abuses of power and the violence that results from this.

First of all, when Francis wrote that his followers are not to appropriate anything (and I think this includes anyone as well [thus addressing both self-centered claims that lead to both greed and lust]), I think he did so because he recognized appropriation to one's self of what belongs to everyone is at the heart of all violence in our relationships. Appropriation is not just about making a claim to property and proprietorship; at its heart, it represents an abusive power-claim. Thus Francis's notion of non-appropriation single-handedly addressed the abuse of power as well as property.

At its heart non-appropriation is about refusing to lay claim to anything; to give up the notion of having a right or a claim to anything. Thus we are not to claim a right to our goods and/or gifts (Adm 5:5-7; 4:2) or reputation (Adm 14:1-4) or life itself (ER 16:10-21), or to judge others (Adm 26:2; ER 2:17). This includes giving up a claim to education (ER 10:7) or even the right to do what is at the heart of our ministry, i.e. preaching (ER 17:4). No one was to grasp at superiorship. We are even not to appropriate to ourselves our own will (LR 10.2). Actually, if we dig deep enough, the only right we should not give up is the right to continue living without rights (see Test 22; ER 16:5). This is so, Julio Micó writes, because: "If we examine closely our ways of acting, we shall always find, hidden somewhere, the sin of appropriation trying to pervert even the most unselfish actions."[40] Furthermore, while, the friars and/or fraternities might actually be allowed to have certain things, even these things were always to be at the service of the poor. As Cajetan Esser wrote years ago in *Repair My House*: "The right of possession then passed to the poorer man, and Francis would have considered it an act of theft to keep the object."[41]

Besides non-appropriation, Francis stressed the need to develop "purity of heart" as a positive way of countering the sins of

---

[40] Julio Micó, O.F.M. Cap., "Franciscan Poverty," *Greyfriars Review* 11.3 (1997): 291.

[41] Cajetan Esser, *Repair My House* (Chicago: Franciscan Herald Press, 1963), 83.

greed and lust. In this, I think he got to the essence of why Jesus stressed purity of heart more than issues around physical purity.[42]

Francis experienced first-hand the breakdown in community when a society develops social codes around the maintenance of physical purity. This was personified in thirteenth century patterns of belonging and non-belonging, purity and uncleanness and other boundary-markers associated with lepers. Francis's embrace of the leper thus represented, as we have seen, a concrete example of the kind of asceticism outlined by Valantis that stood as a counter-cultural stance as well as a new way of relating. However, it was not just a non-appropriation of his society's codes of belonging and non-belonging; he had a positive approach. This is found in his notion of purity of heart; it led him to find solidarity with everyone and everything as the antidote to the sin of the world. A heart full of mercy was free of any hardness of heart toward anyone or any-thing (Adm 27.6). Thus he wrote in the *Earlier Rule*: "But, in the holy love which is God, I beg all my brothers, both the ministers and the others, after overcoming every impediment and putting aside every care and anxiety, to serve, love, honor and adore the Lord God with a clean heart and a pure mind in whatever way they are best able to do so, for that is what He wants above all" (ER, 22.26; 1Frg 15).[43]

In summary, for Francis the "spirit of the flesh" in such vices as greed and lust represented the cause of every sin and vice. To live by the power of the Spirit of the Lord demanded that Francis's followers develop "purity of heart" in a way that empowers us to members of God's Trinitarian household and the new created communal order that this represents.[44]

---

[42] For a development of this notion which links greed, lust and power and the connection to proprietorship, see L. William Countryman, *Dirt, Greed, and Sex: Sexual Ethics in the New Testament and Their Implications for Today*, rev. ed. (Min-neapolis: Fortress, 2007). For a clearer link to the way greed and lust had a deeper connection to "purity of heart" in the Biblical Holiness Codes see Jonathan Kla-wans, *Purity and Sin in Ancient Judaism* (New York: Oxford, 2000).

[43] *FA:ED* 1, 80, 88.

[44] The notion of the way "the Spirit of the Lord" at work among the members of the fraternity/community as opposed to the "works of the flesh" is grounded in Trinitarian relatedness is developed further by Optatus van Asseldonk, O.F.M. Cap., "The Spirit of the Lord and Its Holy Activity in the Writings of Francis," *Greyfriars Review* 5.1 (1991): 126-31, esp. 131.

3) *The parallel call to "take up the cross" as accepting suffering as the consequence of embarking on the way of justice as described in NN. 1 and 2.*

Francis rarely talks about justice itself, especially social justice, in the way we approach it today as the need to challenge or re-order sinful structures. However he seems to make a connection between being a "fraternity-in-mission," as Joe Chinnici calls us, and being persecuted "for the sake of justice" with the notion of non-appropriation when he takes all sorts of scripture quotes in the Earlier Rule and brings them together in Chapter 16 detailing how we are to go "among the Saracens and Other Nonbelievers (ER 16:10-20). He makes an even clearer connection between accepting persecution for justice' sake with the need for "purity of heart" to avoid "envy and greed" and other forms of "solicitude for the world" in the *Later Rule* (LR 10:7-12).

However, within this notion, Francis got to the root of the problem of disordered affections demanding a new evangelical asceticism that would be constituted in justice through his understanding of almsgiving. In the *Earlier Rule* he saw almsgiving as "a legacy and a justice due to the poor that our Lord Jesus Christ acquired for us." Such a form of "acquiring" he identified with non-acquiring or dispossession. By inviting people to give alms, such a reordering became a non-violent way to become dispossessed of one's tendency to proprietorship. Thus the questing brothers would enable a re-distribution of wealth to take place on earth that would insure the eternal reward in heaven for those giving alms on earth: "The brothers who work at acquiring them [alms] will receive a great reward and enable those who give them to gain and acquire one; for all that people leave behind in the world will perish, but they will have a reward from the Lord for the charity and almsgiving they have done" (ER, 9.8-9).[45]

---

[45] The link between suffering persecution for justice with the effort to bringing about justice through almsgiving is also found in the Fragments from Hugh of Digne: 3Frg, 79-81, 92.

THE SCANDAL OF EQUALITY: FRANCISCANS AND WOMEN IN THE THIRTEENTH AND FOURTEENTH CENTURIES AND TODAY

DARLEEN PRYDS

Celano writes in the *Treatise on the Miracles of St. Francis:*

Jacoba dei Settesoli, equal in fame and holiness in the city of Rome, earned the privilege of special love from the saint. It is not for me to repeat, in praise of her, her noble lineage, family honor, and ample wealth, nor the great perfection of her virtues and long, chaste widowhood.

The saint was bedridden with that illness by which, putting off all his weariness, he was about to complete the race with a blessed ending. A few days before his death he decided to send for the Lady Jacoba in Rome, telling her that if she wanted to see the one whom she loved so warmly as an exile, she should come with all haste, because he was about to return to his homeland. A letter was written; a messenger noted for his swiftness was sought and, once found, was outfitted for the journey. Just then there was heard at the door the sound of horses, the commotion of knights, the crowd of an escort. One of the companions, the one who had given instructions to the messenger, went to the door and found there present the one whom he sought because absent. He was struck with wonder and ran very quickly to the saint. Unable to restrain himself for joy, said, 'I have good news for you, father.' Without a pause the saint immediately replied, 'Blessed be God who has brought our Brother Jacoba to us! Open the doors and bring her in. The decree about women is not to be observed for Brother Jacoba.'[1]

This story, related by Thomas of Celano, offers hints at the tender intimacy shared by Lady Jacoba and Francis as evidenced by this, their final meeting. Jacoba, an aristocratic widow from Rome, had heard Francis preaching and sought him out for spiritual guidance specifically on how to offer charity. The two clearly developed a close spiritual relationship, one in which they taught each other the truths of faith. They guided one another in the practice of faith—especially in the practice of being present: being present to one another, and being present to others in need. Theirs was a relationship of mutuality; one could even say it was a relationship of equality.

This passage highlights both the promise and challenge of laity and friars sharing a life of faith. On the one hand the passage from Thomas of Celano's "Treatise on the Miracles of Saint Francis" points to the intimate spiritual relationship that is possible between vowed religious and laity—between men and women. Francis and Jacoba were intensely close in their spiritual rapport; they shared a rapport so close that they intuited their respective needs across long distance and could sense personal presence through closed doors. And yet, Francis had to concede to contemporary norms of comportment and labeled Lady Jacoba a male—and a vowed one at that—by announcing her as "Brother Jacoba." What is the hope for vowed religious and laity to live together in faith when even this sweet and tender story involves the rhetorical manipulation of a lay woman into someone she was not: a vowed religious male?

This paper explores the historical tradition of lay women and their affiliation with the Franciscan friars in the early generations of the Franciscan movement, and turns to the challenges facing all of us today who pretend to share a life of faith across vows and religious status. Looking at four lay women from the early generations of the Franciscan movement—Rose of Viterbo, Angela of

---

[1] Thomas of Celano, "The Treatise on the Miracles of Saint Francis," *Francis of Assisi: Early Documents*, Vol. II, The Founder, ed. Regis Armstrong, O.F.M. Cap., J.A. Wayne Hellmann, O.F.M. Conv., William Short, O.F.M. (New York: New City Press, 2000), 417-18.

Foligno, Margaret of Cortona, and Sancia of Naples—allows us to examine how laity and vowed Franciscans shared spiritual and ministerial commitments. Underlying the examination of these lay Franciscans is one fundamental question: how are lay women who followed and still follow Francis overlooked, ignored, forgotten, or even dismissed as scandalous? There is a strong tradition of lay women who live out Franciscan spirituality at a profound depth; lay women who follow the call of humility and poverty, and from this call provide leadership to their peers.

Why do these followers of Francis so inconsistently appear in the texts, books and surveys of Franciscan history; the pamphlets and retreats on Franciscan spirituality; and even the movies we watch about Francis's story and the tradition he founded? And when they do appear, why do they suddenly and usually so flippantly appear?[2]

The title of my paper suggests my thesis: it remains a scandal to entertain that lay women (and I could add lay men) live out deep spiritual lives that can be mutually educational, beneficial and illuminating to vowed men and women, and especially ordained men—even ordained friars. And yet, a spirituality of mutuality, or as I dared to posit in the title, a spirituality of equality, is one that our world and our Church desperately needs today. It is also one that Francis experimented with in his own life, and we would do well to explore more openly and honestly.

---

[2] One is hard pressed to find mention let alone serious analysis of lay women who were affiliates of the Franciscan order in many text books and overviews of the Franciscans. See for example, Grado Giovanni Merlo, *In the Name of Saint Francis. History of the Friars Minor and Franciscanism until the Early Sixteenth Century*, trans. Raphael Bonnano, O.F.M. (St. Bonaventure, NY: Franciscan Institute Publications, 2009). Maurice Carmody rectifies this tendency somewhat with his inclusion of a chapter on Penitents and designated sections on Rose of Viterbo, Angela of Foligno, and Margaret of Cortona (Sancia of Naples is treated, but only in relation to her husband, Robert of Naples). But Carmody's presentation of these lay Franciscans in a separate chapter emphasizes their separate and discrete role in the tradition and fails to integrate the lay and vowed experience into a mutual commitment. See *The Franciscan Story. St Francis and his Influence since the Thirteenth Century* (London: Athena Press, 2008), see esp. 165-222, 295. Dramatic film presentations of the order's influence equally overlook the role of lay women in the tradition; see for example Liliana Cavani, dir. *Francesco* (1989) which completely overlooks the role of Lady Jacoba at the death of Francis and places Clare instead at his bedside.

This presentation is in two parts. The first part will briefly explore the historical context of the Franciscan spirituality of equality in the early generations of the Franciscan movement. And the second part will very briefly point to the present state of professional ministry in the Church and highlight how far we have gotten from a spirituality of equality that Francis and Lady Jacoba initially forged.

THE MEDIEVAL MODEL OF SPIRITUAL EQUALITY

My recent book, *Women of the Streets: Early Franciscan Women and their Mendicant Vocation* explores the lives of the same four lay women used here from the mid-thirteenth to mid-fourteenth century who affiliated with the Franciscans and carved out lives of faith and spiritual meaning using Francis as their role model.[3] The main purpose of that book was to have lay women included in a series of volumes dedicated to the intellectual life of the Franciscan movement, and thereby to recognize the unique contribution lay women have made to this tradition. The fact that lay women find their way into discussions of the Franciscan movement only in a separate and discrete volume says something about the challenge facing us today. While the influence of lay women affiliated with the Franciscans was widely appreciated and recognized by many of their medieval contemporaries, their work in ministry and their unique interpretations of the Franciscan charism is separated from mainline analyses and discussions of the Franciscan tradition. Other volumes in the series give nod to Clare's contributions to the tradition as the model of female Franciscanism, but rarely include lay women such as Rose of Viterbo as an example of Franciscan evangelism, Angela of Foligno as a prominent teacher of the Franciscan theology, Margaret of Cortona as a pastoral minister in the tradition, or Sancia of Naples as a guardian of the order of friars minor.

---

[3] Darleen Pryds, *Women of the Streets: Early Franciscan Women and their Mendicant Vocation*, The Franciscan Heritage Series 7 (St. Bonaventure, NY: Franciscan Institute Publications, 2010).

Why are these women acknowledged as part of the Franciscan tradition only as special cases in discrete sections or volumes?

I would argue that as a lived community of faith, the Franciscan family still contains vestiges of the thirteenth century anxiety that some friars expressed about interacting with laity, especially lay women. Despite Francis's model of spiritual intimacy with Lady Jacoba, friars in succeeding generations understood all too well the opportunity for scandal that such intimacy could bring.

An anonymous author from the late thirteenth century wrote an academic treatise entitled, "Why Brothers Should not Promote the Order of Penitents."[4] Of special concern was what friars would lose through their interactions with lay women: they would lose their freedom, the author argues. There is no acknowledgement of the wisdom to be gained, the spiritual lessons to be garnered. Instead the author pointed to the possible legal disputes that would develop with lay affiliates, especially over financial or material repercussions. He was worried about gossip that would spread when friars interacted with women, since after all, if the lay woman became pregnant, suspicions about the friars would spread and the resulting scandal would be a distraction to their vocation. Interestingly, the author never expanded on the potential for sexual misconduct among the friars themselves, but instead focused merely on the potential for temptation for lay women.

The author continued his discussion with his concern over meeting with laity in what we might call faith-sharing groups. He argued that the friars would run the risk of being charged with heresy for meeting in private. Rather than embracing the opportunity for his own spiritual growth through meeting with others, he assumed the worst: what if charges were leveled against the friars in question? Scandal could negatively affect the order.

And finally he argued since laity do not take vows of any kind, there would be no way to control or even monitor their behavior either at work or home. Losing control over the behavior of lay affiliates because they did not take vows, the friars would run the risk of being implicated in scandal.

Here lies the dilemma facing friars and vowed religious in the thirteenth century as well as today: the temptation of judging laity

---

[4] For my discussion of this see *Women of the Streets*, 9-11.

as fundamentally different in the seriousness of our spiritual commitments because of the difference in ecclesial status.

To control the vocational focus of the friars and to protect them from the risk of public scandal, this thirteenth century friar argued that the order should have no official connections with laity, especially women. In short, he argued from a place of fear: fear of how scandal could affect the friars without any regard to how scandal could affect the faithful laity, and with no mention given to the wisdom and spiritual mutuality that could be shared.

This anonymous thirteenth century friar stated explicitly what still gets played out in relations between friars and laity: fear prevents real spiritual relationships from developing. But there was no fear between Francis and Jacoba. Instead, they had developed a real relationship: a relationship of trust; a relationship of mutual respect; and a recognition of equality of spiritual gifts: different but equal. How very different from a hierarchical presumption of superiority based on rank, office, ecclesial status, and gender.

The model of spiritual intimacy that Francis and Jacoba forged was imitated in various ways in the lives of four lay women who form the center of my book, *Women of the Streets: Early Franciscan Women and their Mendicant Vocation*: Rose of Viterbo, Angela of Foligno, Margaret of Cortona, and Sancia of Naples. In turning to each one respectively I will amplify what I have said in the book with particular focus on the relationship these women cultivated with friars that allowed them to pursue their ministries and achieve spiritual maturity.

ROSE OF VITERBO

As a street preacher, Rose modeled her particular ministry of evangelization most closely on that of Francis.[5] Taking up her public ministry already as a girl and continuing until her death at the age of 18 in 1251/52, Rose stands out as unique among contemporary laity in her close imitation of Francis and the friars. By dressing in a friar's habit and having her hair cut in a tonsure, she physically

---

[5] This analysis of Rose builds on and presumes what I have already related in Pryds, *Women of the Streets*, 21-32.

appeared like a female friar. By taking to the streets and leading the faithful to the churches of the friars while preaching praises of Jesus and Mary, Rose took up the same public ministry as the friars. And like the friars, she seems to have received implicit clerical permission. One striking feature about the accounts we have of Rose's public evangelization is that there are no references of clerical alarm or concern over it.[6] At a time when scholars, popes, and bishops were debating the legal status of lay preaching, there are no references to clerical concern over Rose's public preaching.[7] Instead there seems to have been a knowing acceptance of the faith-filled speech of this young street-preacher. In fact, there seems to have been a knowing cooperation and trust between local clergy and the preaching girl. Rather than a knee-jerk reaction and presumption of the girl's error in thought and/or deed by clerical authorities including the friars, they allowed Rose to express public leadership that inspired contemporaries and a succession of generations. The suppression of this model of lay female leadership did not come until her canonization in the fifteenth century, after which all official accounts of her piety strike out references to her public evangelization. How might our Church be different if we recognized and promoted the gifts of evangelization among all laity today without fear of the loss of prestige and authority of clergy?

ANGELA OF FOLIGNO

Angela's conversion at middle age launched her career as a spiritual director and widely known theological and spiritual teacher. Until her death in 1309, Angela was known as *magistra theologorum*, or master of theologians. Among the ministries Angela pursued was that of advising friars on their own preaching. As someone "in the pews" so to speak, Angela would have been especially qualified for such a position. But as a lay woman, she could have

---

[6] The hagiographic texts that offer accounts of Rose's ministry are edited by G. Abate, *S. Rosa da Viterbo, Terziana Francescana: Fonti Storiche della Vita e Loro Revisione Critica* (Rome: Editrice Miscellanea Francescana, 1952).

[7] For a brief discussion on the twelfth and thirteenth century debates over lay preaching, see Pryds, *Women of the Streets*, 11-14.

been dismissed as a pest by the friars. Indeed her more expressive outbursts at the Basilica of St. Francis did cause a stir among the friars who requested she not be allowed to return.[8] While Angela's passionately expressive piety embarrassed some friars, her wisdom, honesty, and deep understanding of Franciscan theology made her widely known and sought after for advice. Whether or not friars actually sought her advice on their own pastoral leadership, she offered it, as is seen from various letters in which she told friars how to preach effectively and how to maintain integrity in ministry.

> When one of you preaches, hears confessions, or gives counsel, he should not keep his mind on creatures, but on the Creator. Do not behave like fools, for whatever the fool has his eye on, there is his whole heart. When you come across flatterers, men or women, who tell you 'Brother, your words have converted me to penance,' do not pay any attention to them but rather turn to the Creator and thank him for this blessing. There are many preachers of falsehoods whose preaching is full of greed, and out of greed they preach for honors, money, and fame. My beloved sons, I wish with all my heart that you preach the holy truth and that the book you rely on be the God-man. I do not tell you to give up your books, but that you should always be willing to do this, whether you keep them or abandon them. I do not want you to be like those who preach only with words of learning and dryly report the deeds of saints, but rather speak about them with the same divine savor as they had who performed these deeds. Those who have first preached well to themselves with this divine savor know how to preach well to others.[9]

Her advice was direct and clear. Implicitly the advice was issued from a relationship of trust and mutual respect with the friars; otherwise Angela would have been dismissed as a nuisance and busy-body. Her spiritual wisdom was grounded in fervent prayer

---

[8] Pryds, *Women of the Streets*, 33-47, esp. 41 for her emotional piety.

[9] Paul Lachance, trans. *Angela of Foligno. Complete Works*, Classics of Western Spirituality (New York: Paulist Press, 1993), 261-62.

and devotional practices, so that her words of advice were taken seriously. How would our Church be different if clergy took seriously the counsel and advice of wise laity today?

MARGARET OF CORTONA

Margaret of Cortona was known at one time as the third light of the Franciscans, alluding to her leadership among the lay affiliates of the order, yet she is hardly remembered today except in rather tight circles of the Franciscan devoted.[10] Yet after her adult conversion to a life of faith, Margaret became such a prominent leader in the city of Cortona that lay women flocked to her for pastoral support and ministerial needs until her death in 1297. She was the minister of choice for contemporary lay women who brought their infants to her for baptism, a custom well known in the middle ages, but one that increasingly rankled friars whose prominence and importance were threatened by Margaret's popularity. While she worked alongside the friars for a time, her close rapport with them strained as her popularity among the laity rose. In addition, her proximity to the friars allowed her to advise them much as Angela of Foligno did. She especially counseled the friars on how to be effective preachers: focus on the Gospels and Pauline letters and don't be too chatty.[11] In this case, however, the close rapport soured over time. There is clear evidence from a chapter meeting of the friars that some of the friars were concerned about Margaret's prominence, and disagreed over her holiness. Her affiliation with the friars proved to be more trouble than it was worth given the level of dissension that her importance brought into the Franciscan community. She eventually departed ways with the friars and took up in a hermitage attached to a diocesan church, where her fame as a sage, holy woman continued to inspire the people of Cortona.

Margaret's story provides the nuance needed to understand the association of lay women with the friars: such a rapport was rarely easy going and without human flaws. Yet we see in this case

---

[10] For an overview of her life, see my *Women of the Streets*, 49-61.

[11] Pryds, *Women of the Streets*, 58.

how a lay woman persevered in her own ministry and life of prayer rather than relinquish her sense of self and vocation for any sense of safety and well-being the relationship with the friars may have offered. She had grown into her own unique sense of self and call-ing, and followed that call. How might our Church be different if laity consistently listened to and followed their own call in minis-try and faith?

SANCIA OF NAPLES

Sancia is the least known of the women I discuss in *Women of the Streets*, and is usually treated only in relation to her husband, Robert, King of Naples.[12] Sancia herself highlighted this part-nership of power when she could gain leverage from it, yet she was an independent woman with her own sense of vocation and self.[13] During her reign as queen of an expansive kingdom that spread from the south of France to the end of the boot of Italy, and technically included other territories, Sancia carved out a role as guardian of religious life for the friars and imposed her concerns and will on the order so that the friars turned to her for support and received from her advice which they often took. In particular her concern was with how the friars lived out their vow of poverty, and she counseled the friars as a mother would counsel her sons:

> [A] mother loves her sons, and so I love my sons, the Friars Minor ... Sancia, by the grace of God, queen of Jerusa-lem and Sicily [Naples], your humble servant and devoted daughter sends greetings in the Lord Jesus Christ.[14]

With these words, Sancia addressed the General Chapter of the Franciscan Order that met in Paris in 1329. She chose particu-larly warm and maternal language to position herself as a particular patron of the order. Not merely a patron who offered material support or political support, although she did offer both, Sancia

---

[12] Pryds, *Women of the Streets*, 63-75.
[13] Pryds, *Women of the Streets*, 69.
[14] Pryds, *Women of the Streets*, 63.

offered what no man could: the love and support of a mother. She wielded this image of mother to inform and influence the friars on matters of policy within the order. Without a doubt her royal office allowed her to impose her will on the order, but her method of presenting her ideas, concerns, and personal preferences was to couch her power in the image as mother. In this intimate role, Sancia gave voice to her views on how the friars should live according to their vows, as an adviser who saw them falling away from their ideals. While the friars did not always agree with her, they respected her and often deferred to her. How might our Church be different if laity helped administer some institutions run by vowed religious?

These four snapshots of lessons taken from the early generations of the Franciscan movement could be written differently with a number of different lessons and questions posed based on the subtle nuances found in the lives of these women. The point here is merely to demonstrate the depth and complexity of lay women's interactions with the friars that are usually overlooked and ignored in studies and discussions of the movement. In short, relationship based on presence to one another is a feature of the Franciscan tradition, and yet it does not always come through in how we present the tradition ... or even how we live it today.

FRANCISCAN SPIRITUALITY FOR TODAY'S CHURCH

In 2007 at this symposium, Joseph Chinnici delivered a paper on the impact of clericalization on Franciscan Evangelization. He opened with a poignant story of faith.[15] A fellow friar had hit a point of complacency and routine in his ministry in the years following the second Vatican council. As the nature of ministry changed to one of collaboration with lay people, he felt at a loss of what to do and how to be in ministry. One day a young woman in her mid-thirties came to him asking for instruction to enter the

---

[15] Joseph P. Chinnici, O.F.M., "The Impact of Clericalization on Franciscan Evangelization," in *Franciscan Evangelization. Striving to Preach the Gospel*, ed. Elise Saggau, O.S.F., Washington Theological Union Symposium Papers, 2007 (St. Bonaventure, NY: Franciscan Institute Publications, 2008), 79-122, at 79-80.

Church. "I hardly believed what I taught, but dutifully I read the new catechism with her ..." She was received into the Church, was baptized and received First Communion. And the friar went on, as if in a dull fog of malaise.

Six months later, the woman appeared again, this time relating to the priest that she had been diagnosed with leukemia and would die in six months. She requested the friar bring her communion each week. He agreed, but thought, "it won't do much good." After several months, she asked him if he would stay to talk with her in addition to giving her the Blessed Sacrament. He said yes, but thought, "What could I possibly say?"

When he showed up for this conversation, the young woman said the following to him:

> Father, I know you cannot do much for me; and I do not want you to speak; just listen. You have done everything for me: educated me in the faith, talked to me about God, baptized me into Christ's Body, and now for five months, given me the bread of Life. I am so grateful, Father, so, so grateful. This communion with Christ has been my salvation. And I am at peace. I want you to know that from the time I was diagnosed with leukemia, I decided to offer up my sufferings for the continuation and fruitfulness of your priesthood. Thank you, so much.[16]

Chinnici concluded the introduction of his article by remarking:

> If we catch this story, we catch the definition of Church in our Franciscan tradition, its reality as a partnership, "in the manner of giving and receiving." [a quote from Bonaventure] its Trinitarian focus on the exchange of grace, communion and spiritual and material goods.
>
> If we catch this story, we catch also why the clericalization of the mission of the friars and its correlate have been such an obstacle to our evangelical way of life in the Church and in the world. We catch finally a luminous ex-

---

[16] Chinnici, "Impact of Clericalization," 80.

ample of the path we need to make straight in the world from our present to our future.[17]

Inherent in this story and in Chinnici's evaluation of it is the evidence of ministry as mutual service and the ruin, or at the very least, emptiness that develops from misguided clericalism. The presumption of clerical primacy and unilateral authority can seduce clerics into a ministry that lacks faith and conviction and breeds in them elements of malaise and non-engagement. Fundamentally, fear is cultivated in such an environment. Often this develops as fear of lay women.

In 2005 the U.S. Bishops published statistics that confirmed what anyone knows who goes into a Catholic church regularly.[18] Of the growing number of lay ecclesial ministers who work in the church, the vast majority of them are lay women (68%) [20% lay men; 16% religious women). And yet the men entering the priesthood and educated after 1980 show a decreasing willingness or interest "in working with lay ministers as equals."[19] One can't help but wonder if fear is at the root of this decreasing willingness and interest to work with lay ministers.

The interpersonal problems and challenges for ministry that these statistics point to could find part of their solution in the medieval Franciscan approach to ministry and faith formation forged by Francis and Jacoba, and implemented in the early generations of Franciscan life by Rose, Angela, Margaret and Sancia. When the complexities of our historical tradition are forgotten, it would be easy to overlook the radical mutual engagement and equality that lay women and friars experienced and experimented with in the first century of the order. But returning to a mere recognition of such a tradition could be a wake up call to laity and clergy alike in these present days.

People often ask me why I am a medievalist. The answer is simple: the models of lay leadership are inspiring to me. To study

---

[17] Chinnici, "Impact of Clericalization," 81.

[18] Chinnici, "Impact of Clericalization," 90; from USCCB, "Co-Workers in the Vineyard of the Lord," *Origins* 25 (Dec. 1, 2005), 408-09.

[19] Chinnici, "Impact of Clericalization," 97, from Dean Hoge and Jacqueline Wenger, *Evolving Visions of the Priesthood: Changes from Vatican II to the Turn of the New Century* (Collegeville: Liturgical Press, 2003), 69.

lay women who perceived their vocations in ministry and worked alongside clergy as equals seems to me a profound lesson worth spending my life to explore and bring back into today's world and today's church. As scandalous as it is, a shared life of faith between people of all walks of life is inherent in the tradition I choose to follow: the Franciscan tradition.

A Franciscan Economy

Vincent Cushing, O.F.M.

At the outset I am keenly aware that a basic question is whether there is such an entity as a "Franciscan economy." The correct answer is negative. However, I do believe there is a sound foundation for saying there is a distinctly Franciscan approach to the economy and how we participate in it. The world of economic theory is indeed complex, far beyond what this paper's author can address. Nevertheless, there is within the Franciscan movement an ongoing desire to clarify how the Franciscan movement envisions a particular style of living and spirituality that Franciscans embrace. Elements of that style include, but are not restricted to: following the Gospel, care for the poor and powerless, simplicity of life in clothing, food, housing, and parenting. Equally important is enjoyment of and careful attention to the beauty and care of creation. Finally, active participation and support of social justice from the standpoint of our Christian ethic of love and humility serves as the foundation for Franciscan engagement in contemporary issues both local and global. These are relatively simple approaches to describe, yet quite demanding in one's daily life.

Nevertheless the subject of a "Franciscan economy" is a daunting one. I wrestled with the focus of this talk – is it about how we Franciscans face the demands of our economy? Does it address whether we believe in any sense in contemporary western capitalism? Or, is it about how we are expected to be countercultural within the contemporary economic ethos?

This task is contemporary (can anyone doubt that the economy is perhaps the most pressing issue in the U.S. in the year 2010) and also intriguing – does the Franciscan movement historically shed any light on the contemporary issues we face? My presentation in response to these queries contains three elements. The task before us calls for a realistic evaluation of the Franciscan role in American society. Is it visionary and operative? Do we witness to a Franciscan vision of social justice and how it can serve to support the change in the way we live and think, help provide an opportunity to reevaluate our mission and ministries, and aid in reviewing our own personal dedication and communal living?

First, I describe one element of Franciscan history that sheds light on how the Franciscan tradition of the past can shape and influence our approach in the present. Secondly, I reflect on contemporary papal teaching on the economy to serve as a foundation for our contemporary Franciscan approach. Thirdly, I offer conclusions to help articulate our own spirituality in the face of the challenges to social justice in our day.

We need to avoid assuming the economies operative in early and medieval Franciscan movement offer a response to today's issues. Indeed, they were markedly different from current models. Clearly, they are not simply replicated in our day. Rather, our task is both to understand the history and to see what spiritual values it suggests to us that might prove helpful today.

One of the most successful ventures of the Franciscan movement emerged in the late Middle Ages and Renaissance. Known as the *Montes Pietatis*,[1] they served to alleviate the heavy burden of interest charges on the lending of money. With interest ranging from 40 to 80%, borrowing was virtually impossible. Nevertheless, with the rise of the merchant and artisan classes the need to borrow money intensified. The Franciscans inaugurated, in truth borrowed, and developed this cooperative arrangement in cities throughout Europe, offering a practical solution to a real problem. Various theologians and canonists disagreed with the Franciscans, but their creative solution to a real problem continued and grew for over a century and eventually gained papal approval. The ques-

---

[1] *Montes Pietatis* are credit organizations that lend money at low rates of interest, or without interest at all, upon the security of objects left in pawn, with a view to protecting persons in want from usurers. Being charitable establishments, they lend only to people who are in need of funds to pass through some financial crisis, as in cases of general scarcity of food, misfortunes, etc. On the other hand, these institutions do not seek financial profit, but use all profits that may accrue to them for the payment of employees and to extend the scope of their charitable work. *Montes Pietatis*, New Advent CD Rom, "Catholic Encyclopedia."

tion of interest on lending money, known as usury, was a fiercely debated issue, with many canonists and theologians viewing it as an "unnatural" – and therefore evil use of money. The Franciscans disagreed, insisting that their approach was the lesser of two evils. Today we would call them credit unions.

I am not so interested in the mechanics of the *Montes Pietatis* so much as understanding the underlying attitudes that prompted this good work. To achieve this the Franciscans must have understood the economy of that day, appreciated its limitations, and devised a practical solution that helped many borrowers. Hence, their approach was knowledgeable, sensitive, and helpful. In a word, it was pastoral, but pastoral with a view to correcting a serious burden in the society of that day. As such it offers a paradigm for action today in its values and methodology: knowledge of the situation, awareness of the needs of the people, practical in its proposed response.

In approaching issues of social justice and the economy today the need for sound information and accurate data is paramount. Our fellow Christians who disagree with our approaches to social justice most often accuse us of not adequately understanding the contemporary issues of justice and economy and of not paying sufficient attention to all of the data that pertains to the situation we are addressing. In a sense they accuse us of being naïve, ignorant, or, even worse, of not exercising due diligence.

Moreover, those who disagree with us often characterize our thinking as lacking an awareness of the implications of the policy we advocate, insisting we are insensitive to the impact policies will have in other related arenas. Hence, we see a need both for sufficient knowledge of the issues we address, and also a sound theological foundation for our advocacy. This requires us to go beyond our Franciscan heritage, and to seek a robust theological foundation for our views, one that both respects our Franciscan charism while also anchoring us in mainstream Christian theology.

The recent encyclical of Benedict XVI *Caritas in Veritate*[2] continues the papal custom of offering a Catholic view on contemporary issues of justice and economics. Benedict sees the issues of justice, peace, and economic justice shaped by Christian eschatology as the fulfillment of the human situation in the Kingdom of God.

---

[2] *Caritas in Veritate*, Vatican.VA/brn-xv1 enc, June 29, 2009.

Secondly, his thought on Jesus as a Messiah of peace and justice in the Synoptic Gospels equally anchors his treatment of justice in the world.

Perhaps the strongest theological foundation for the worldwide ministry of justice and peace, and especially for economic justice, is rooted in the theology of the Kingdom of God. This central focus of Jesus' preaching highlights the "world-changing" agenda of Jesus as the eschatological prophet of a new age. As such, it includes a number of issues that should be characteristic of contemporary social justice ministry. Among these are the following:

- The understanding that the church exists to bring about the kingdom of God in the world. This should be seen in the depth and range of the Kingdom. It means much more than claiming the church should continue to do what it normally does, but it should now include and emphasize a social justice agenda. Rather, it means that the *raison d'être* of the church is that it is in mission to the entire world to bring about a kingdom, a reign, a governance of peace and justice. This is a basic re-orientation of our notion of church. The Kingdom is central and the church is its servant. From this a host of theological claims follow.

- In this understanding the efforts of the church are first directed to the whole world in a Gospel message of peace, but it is to a whole world that is experienced in a local and historical setting. Given the urgency of this message a major effort is called for locally as to how the church will communicate to the world(s) we live in. This necessarily carries within it the notion that the church is experienced locally and pastorally. In turn, this calls on the church to understand the culture it lives in on the local level and to engage in focused social and cultural analysis. Only after this effort is the local church in an informed position to analyze what is going on and to begin to design a suitable agenda for action. The setting of agenda is not confined solely to social and cultural analysis; this analysis is subsequently engaged in prolonged and thoughtful conversation with the Gospel and the entire Judaeo-Christian tradition.

- This approach evokes a key role of the church and its members, a role that is prophetic and not restricted to its clergy and religious. A prophet is one who can interpret the history of the age in terms of how God is calling his people to action. A prophet or a band of prophets are (com)missioned to pronounce where God's agenda is breaking into human history and to galvanize the action needed to support justice and peace. They need to be informed and effective.

- This understanding of kingdom, church, and prophecy resituates the role of laity in the church and returns to the ancient notion that all in the church are disciples called to action and the witness of prophetic Christian living and vocation. No longer do the previous categories of laity and clergy and their rather "segregated" boundaries adequately handle this deeper awareness of the discipleship of all Christians, Catholic and Protestant. Those boundaries are the markings of a past church, and their somewhat anemic theology of the laity is laid to rest in this understanding. Indeed, the theology of the laity touched on, but virtually ignored, in Vatican II is its description of "secularity" as the enduring characteristic of laity describing where and how the ministry of justice and peace takes place.

- Furthermore, the notion of the kingdom of God sheds light on what pastoral ministry is about. In this understanding ministry is clearly and accurately described as equipping the saints both for their lives as Christians in the world as well as their interior spiritual life. In simple terms it is built on a sound understanding of the inauguration and commissioning of disciples in baptism, their strengthening in the Spirit in being confirmed in the faith and their understanding on what being a disciple entails. It looks to a "secular" spirituality that addresses the two basic expressions of adult human existence: how and where we work and our expression of human sexuality in marriage and family or as dedicated single people.

Turning now to the practice of economic justice in our day we find apt resources for consideration. Of particular value is the Franciscan Action Network based in Washington, DC. In one of the Network's "white papers" on economic justice Father David Couturier, O.F.M. Cap., directly addresses the contemporary economic dilemma the US is currently experiencing. He offers basic guidelines for Franciscan communities and congregations (including secular Franciscan fraternities):

> ... it is time to take another look at the Franciscan tradition for help in developing a more relational economic paradigm for the Twenty-first Century. In my book I outline five principles that we believe can help us construct a more relational experience of economic activity than is presently displayed in the 'pick yourself up by your own bootstrap' idiom of aggressive capitalism. The five principles are:

> - *Transparency* – mutuality in all things. All the goods, economic activities, and ministerial activities are at the service of the whole. There are no hidden schemes by leadership or membership.
> - *Equity* – Individuals and communities get what they need and contribute what they have for the common good and the building up of communion. Service replaces entitlement.
> - *Participation* – Build mechanism of cooperation and communion of persons without domination or deprivation.
> - *Solidarity* – Those who have more give more to those deprived. All work to undo structures of sin that serve as obstacles to communion.

- *Austerity* – The minimum necessary, not the maximum allowed, so that others can simply live and work.[3]

What becomes clear in these principles is that the quest for a "Franciscan economy" needs first to be realized within the Franciscan family itself. This is a return to the basic theological principle that orthopraxy precedes orthodoxy, or that it is not enough to talk the talk, it's necessary to walk the walk. Franciscan, Christian witness that is both pastoral and sensitive and that emerges from the lived experience of Franciscan communities is the surest way to build a Franciscan economy.

---

[3] David B. Couturier, O.F.M. Cap., Franciscan Action Network, 2009, as found in Couturier "Hope and Security: New Foundations," *Horizon*, 32:1 (Fall, 2006): 11-16.

ABOUT THE AUTHORS

JOSEPH NANGLE, O.F.M., presently serves as the treasurer and secretary for the Board of Directors of the Franciscan Action Network. Rev. Nangle has previously been involved in missionary work in Latin America and has recently retired from Franciscan Mission Service (FMS) in Washington, DC, of which he was a co-founder. A member of the Franciscan Friars of Holy Name Province he currently ministers to the Hispanic community at Our Lady Queen of Peace Parish in Arlington, VA. He has lived at the Assisi Community, an intentional community in inner city Washington, DC, for the past twenty-two years. Consisting of two vowed members and a number of lay women and men, the community strives for a simple lifestyle while engaging in a variety of activities and ministries for social change.

MICHAEL CROSBY, O.F.M. CAP. lives in community with other friars in a downtown Milwaukee parish that serves the urban poor, homeless and marginalized. His own ministry revolves around his attempt to proclaim the gospel of God's Trinitarian reign and the conversion that is needed to bring about Trinitarian relationships of equality at all levels "on earth as it is in heaven." Specifically it attempts to help develop a spirituality of discipleship for U.S. and other "First World" Catholics. This effort has two main expressions: corporate reform and church reform.

He was influential in getting Catholics to work with the Protestant and Jewish communities at the Interfaith Center on Corporate Responsibility (ICCR). He has been very involved in a wide range of issues—from South Africa and infant formula to global warming and tobacco control. He coordinates the work of religious institutions in the Wisconsin, Iowa and Minnesota, Dakotas (WIM/CRI) who are part of the ICCR.

DARLEEN PRYDS, Ph.D., is a Catholic laywoman, especially interested in teaching and researching historical cases of lay religious leadership. She has published several articles and a book on lay preaching within the Medieval Church. In addition to teaching at the Franciscan School of Theology at Berkeley, Darleen has received many research grants, including a Fulbright Fellowship to Italy; a Research Fellowship at the Medieval Institute at the University of Notre Dame; and a National Endowment for the Humanities Research grant to research at the Vatican Film Library at Saint Louis University. She remains a loyal alumna of her alma mater, USC, and loves watching USC football games.

VINCENT CUSHING, O.F.M. served a long and distinguished term as the President of the Washington Theological Union in Washington D.C. and now teaches ecclesiology on the faculty there. He is a pastpresident of the Association of Theological Schools in the United States and Canada and President Emeritus of Washington Theological Union.

NEW TITLES FROM
FRANCISCAN INSTITUTE PUBLICATIONS

COLETTE OF CORBIE (1381-1447)
LEARNING AND HOLINESS
by Elisabeth Lopez and translated by Joanna
Waller. In 1994, Elisabeth Lopez published,
in French, a serious study of Colette and
her reform movement. With a translation
by Joanna Waller, this important work is
appearing for the first time in English. 640
pages, Hardcover, Size: 6 x 9,
ISBN: 1-57659-217-0, $50.00.

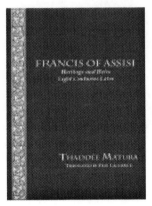

FRANCIS OF ASSISI:
HERITAGE AND HEIRS
EIGHT CENTURIES LATER
by Thaddée Matura, O.F.M. Translated by
Paul Lachance, O.F.M. A fresh examination
of how the Franciscan tradition has adapted
and contemporized over 800 years. 112
pages, Tradepaper, Size: 6 x 9,
ISBN: 1-57659-214-6, $25.00.

FRANCISCAN INSTITUTE PUBLICATIONS
3261 WEST STATE STREET
ST. BONAVENTURE, NY 14778 USA
WWW.FRANCISCANPUBLICATIONS.COM
PHONE: 716-375-2062
FAX: 716-375-2113
E-MAIL: FIP@SBU.EDU

RECENT RELEASES

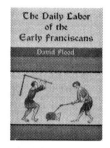

THE DAILY LABOR OF THE EARLY FRAN-
CISCANS by David Flood, O.F.M., released
2010. Told from the vantage point of an his-
torian, Flood leads the reader through his
analysis of the early movement. 148 pages,
ISBN: 1-57659-156-5, $30.00.

RULE OF THE FRIARS MINOR, 1209-2009:
HISTORICAL PERSPECTIVES, LIVED RE-
ALITIES. Released 2010. This volume presents six scholarly essays and nine interven-
tions by friars who live the rule in diverse
cultural, national and religious contexts. 180
pages, ISBN: 1-57659-212-X, $20.00.

REJOICING IN THE WORKS OF THE
LORD: BEAUTY IN THE FRANCISCAN
TRADITION by Mary Beth Ingham, C.S.J.
Released 2010. This volume focuses on the
appreciation of beauty in the writings of Bonaventure of Bagnoregio and John Duns Scotus. 78 Pages, ISBN: 1-57659-205-7. $5.00.

WOMEN OF THE STREETS, EARLY
FRANCISCAN WOMEN AND THEIR MEN-
DICANT VOCATION by Darleen Pryds. Released 2010. Rose of Viterbo, Angela of Foligno, Margaret of Cortona and Sancia, Queen
of Naples pursued their religious vocation in
the first century of the Franciscan Order. 84
pages, ISBN: 1-57659-206-5. $5.00.

Franciscan Institute Publications
www.franciscanpublications.com
Phone: 716-375-2062
Fax: 716-375-2113
E-mail: fip@sbu.edu

COMING SOON
FROM FRANCISCAN INSTITUTE PUBLICATIONS

DYING, AS A FRANCISCAN: APPROACHING OUR TRAN-
SITUS TO ETERNAL LIFE ACCOMPANYING OTHERS
ON THE WAY TO THEIRS. Spirit and Life Series 15. The pro-
ceedings of the Ninth National Franciscan Forum features presentations by Thomas Nairn, O.F.M., Mary Petrosky, F.M.M., Kath-
erine McCarron, O.S.F., Michael F. Cusato, O.F.M. and Daniel
Sulmasy, O.F.M. Available March 2011.

WORDS MADE FLESH: ESSAYS HONORING KENAN B.
OSBORNE, O.F.M. This volume contains papers by Bill Short,
Allan Wolter, Zachary Hayes, Regis Duffy, Michael Guinan, Jo-
hannes Freyer, Antonie Vos, and Mary Beth Ingham, with topics
ranging from Old Testament to Bonaventure, Duns Scotus, a work
by Riccerio of Muccia, a Franciscan theology of the Word and the
Franciscan tradition in the third millennium. Available May 2011.

Peter of John Olivi, COMMENTARY ON MARK, translation by
Robert Karris. Largely ignored until recently due to conflict with
both Church and Order, Olivi may be considered one of the most
original and interesting philosophers of the later Middle Ages.
For most of his life (1248-1298) he taught at Franciscan houses
of study in southern France and Florence, but is perhaps better
known for his connection with the so-called "Spiritual" reform.
Available May 2011.

STUDIES IN EARLY FRANCISCAN SOURCES: THE WRIT-
INGS OF FRANCIS AND CLARE OF ASSISI, edited by Mi-
chael W. Blastic, O.F.M., Jay Hammond, Ph.D., and J.A. Wayne
Hellmann, O.F.M. Conv. This first volume, in three parts: The
Rules and Admonitions, The Letters and Prayers, and Writings
of Clare, presents the latest research by noted scholars and au-
thors Luigi Pellegrini, Jean François Godet-Calogeras, Bill Short,
Michael Blastic, Michael Cusato, Jay Hammond, Laurent Gallant,
J.A. Wayne Hellmann, Ingrid Peterson and Lezlie Knox. Available
May 2011.

THE WTU SYMPOSIUM SERIES

GREED, LUST, AND POWER: FRANCISCAN STRATEGIES FOR
BUILDING A MORE JUST WORLD (2010)
ISBN: 1-57659-220-0   14.00

POVERTY AND PROSPERITY: FRANCISCANS AND THE USE OF
MONEY (2009)   ISBN: 1-57659-158-1 $14.00

MORAL ACTION IN A COMPLEX WORLD:
FRANCISCAN PERSPECTIVES (2008)
ISBN: 1-57659-154-9 $14.00

ᛁ FRANCISCAN EVANGELIZATION:
STRIVING TO PREACH THE GOSPEL (2007)
ISBN: 1-57659-148-4 $14.00

FRANCISCANS AND LITURGICAL LIFE: LET US PRAISE, ADORE
AND GIVE THANKS (2006)
ISBN: 1-57659-141-7 $14.00

FRANCISCANS AND THE SCRIPTURES:
LIVING THE WORD OF GOD (2005)
ISBN: 1-57659-138-7 $14.00

"GO REBUILD MY HOUSE":
FRANCISCANS AND THE CHURCH TODAY (2004)
ISBN: 1-57659-194-8 $14.00

FRANCISCANS AND CREATION:
WHAT IS OUR RESPONSIBILITY? (2003)
ISBN: 1-57659-190-5 $12.00

FRANCISCAN IDENTITY AND POSTMODERN CULTURE (2002)
ISBN: 1-57659-186-7 $12.00

THE FRANCISCAN INTELLECTUAL TRADITION (2001)
ISBN: 1-57659-180-8 $12.00

AVAILABLE FROM FRANCISCAN INSTITUTE PUBLICATIONS
Phone: 716-375-2062   Fax: 716-375-2113   E-mail: fip@sbu.edu